the
japanese
kitchen

the
japanese
kitchen

DELICATE DISHES FROM AN ELEGANT CUISINE

Masaki Ko

LORENZ BOOKS

This edition published by Lorenz Books

LORENZ BOOKS are available for bulk purchase for sales promotion and for premium use. For details, write or call the sales director, Lorenz Books, 27 West 20th Street, New York, NY 10011; (800) 354-9657

Lorenz Books is an imprint of Anness Publishing Inc.

Publisher: Joanna Lorenz
Senior Cookbook Editor: Linda Fraser
Designer: Ian Sandom
Jacket Design: Balley Design Associates
Photographer: Juliet Piddington
Stylist: Marion Price
Food for photography: Carol Tennant
Illustrator: Madeleine David

Front cover: Nicki Dowey, Photographer and Stylist;
Angela Boggiano, Home Economist

Previously published as *Creative Cooking Library: Taste of Japan*

Printed and bound in Hong Kong/China

1 3 5 7 9 10 8 6 4 2

CONTENTS

INTRODUCTION

THE PHILOSOPHY OF JAPANESE COOKING

Japanese cuisine is an orchestrated symphony of art. The style of cooking is simple but simplicity is the most difficult characteristic to achieve. The Japanese cook respects individual ingredients and prepares them with care to ensure that each flavour is brought out in the dish.

COOKING METHODS

Fresh raw ingredients are used for dishes such as the famous *Sushi* and *Sashimi*, where the skill is in the preparation of the food rather than literally in the cooking method.

Another widely practised technique is that of grilling. As a fish-eating nation, much care is taken over perfecting this. It is very important to grill food well to ensure that it retains its flavour and stays moist without being adversely affected by the fierce heat or by the burning charcoal.

Finally, boiling in various types of stock is another classic Japanese cooking method. These dishes are warming and nutritious. They are usually served bubbling in earthenware pots and guests are often invited to serve themselves.

SEASONING

The Japanese alphabet is made up of a series of consonants followed by vowels. For example, the way to express the "S" characters is sa, shi, su, se and so. This also happens to relate to the seasonings used in Japan. The following shows the exact order in which seasonings are applied to dishes, based on scientifically proven logic. The theory is that bigger particles, such as sugar, cannot penetrate foods when obstructed by smaller particles, such as salt. The following seasonings should always be used in a correct sequence as shown here.

Sa stands for *sato* which is sugar. This is widely used in marinades and sauces.

Shi stands for *shio* or salt.

Su stands for *su*, vinegar, which evaporates when heated and loses its flavour. So it is vital that this is not added too early in the cooking process.

Se stands for *shoyu* or *seuyu*, which is soy sauce. This seasoning is also likely to lose its flavour if added too early; therefore it is added near the end of cooking and/or used to flavour food just before it is eaten.

So stands for miso paste and this flavouring is used to impart added flavour to many dishes.

1 Ready-mixed sushi vinegar 2 Sake 3 Okonomiyaki sauce 4 Tamari soy sauce 5 Japanese curry powder 6 Gari 7 Bonito flakes 8 Usukuchi soy sauce 9 Mirin 10 Rice vinegar 11 Soy sauce 12 Takuwan 13 Tonkatsu sauce 14 Kombu seaweed 15 Wasabi paste 16 Umeboshi 17 Katakuri-ko 18 Miso paste

Basic Recipes

BOILED RICE

Washing rice is very important as it improves the flavour of the cooked rice. The amount of water the rice is cooked in can be increased slightly depending on the preferred texture of the cooked rice and if you know that the grains are old crop rather than new crop. In some recipes part of the measured quantity of water is replaced with some flavouring.

Serves 4-6
480g/1lb 1oz/2⅓ cups rice
600ml/1 pint/2½ cups water

1 Place the rice in a large bowl. Pour plenty of water over it, then quickly drain this water away, otherwise a bran smell will remain after cooking.

2 Stir the grains well, firmly pressing the rice by hand to remove all bran powder. Pour plenty of water over the rice and quickly drain it away. Repeat this three or four times.

3 Then add plenty of water and stir by hand two or three times. Drain the water away. Repeat two or three times, until the water runs clear.

4 Drain the rice well through a fine strainer and leave it to drain for 30-60 minutes.

5 Transfer the rice to a rice cooker, add the measured water and switch on. Alternatively, use a deep saucepan, cover and cook over a moderate heat until steam comes out. Reduce the heat and simmer for 10-12 minutes. Do not open the pan during cooking. Finally, before removing the lid, cook the rice over a high heat for 5 seconds.

6 When the rice is cooked, leave it to stand for 15 minutes, then remove the lid and stir the rice once with a wet spatula to remove excess vapour (use a wet spatula in order to prevent the rice from sticking to it). Serve immediately.

NIBOSHI – OR IRIKO – DASHI

This is a stock for miso soup and everyday use.

Makes about 800ml/27fl oz/3½ cups
20g/¾ oz niboshi or iriko (small dried sardines for stock)
5g/⅛ oz kombu seaweed (optional)

1 Tear away the belly and head of the niboshi or iriko, as they make the stock bitter, then tear in half vertically.

2 Add the niboshi to 900ml/ 1½ pints/3¾ cups cold water. For added flavour, add the kombu seaweed and leave to soak for 10 minutes. Heat the stock, then reduce the heat just before it boils. Do not boil. Skim the stock carefully to clear. Simmer for 15 minutes. If using kombu, simmer for only 5 minutes, remove from the heat and leave to stand for 5 minutes.

3 Line a strainer with paper towel and place it over a large bowl, then gently strain the stock.

INSTANT STOCK

For speed or convenience when you need a small amount of stock, granules are very good. They are very popular in Japan, and you can find many varieties in Japanese supermarkets. For example, *hondashi* are kombu seaweed and bonito flake stock granules; *iriko-dashi* are niboshi or iriko stock granules; concentrated kombu seaweed and bonito flake stock is available in liquid form; and there is also a tea-bag style instant stock. These are all useful for miso soup and everyday cooking. Follow the packet instructions.

KOMBU SEAWEED AND BONITO FLAKE STOCK

This popular stock, known as *Ichiban-dashi* is used for delicately flavoured dishes.

Makes about 800ml/27fl oz/3½ cups
10 x 15cm/4 x 6in piece dried kombu seaweed (about 10g/¼ oz)
10-15g/¼ -½ oz bonito flakes

1 Wipe the kombu seaweed with a damp cloth and cut two slits in it with scissors, so that it flavours the stock effectively.

2 Soak the kombu in 900ml/ 1½ pints/3¾ cups cold water for at least 30 minutes, preferably for 1 hour.

3 Heat the kombu in its soaking water over a moderate heat. Just before the water boils, remove the seaweed, otherwise the stock will be dulled. Add the bonito flakes and bring to the boil over a high heat, then remove the pan from the heat.

4 Leave the stock until all the bonito flakes have sunk to the bottom of the pan. Line a strainer with paper towel or muslin and place it over a large bowl, then gently strain the stock.

INGREDIENTS

ADUKI BEANS Small, red sweet beans, used in desserts, also available in glacé form (*ama-natto*) or in a paste (*neri-an*).

BEANCURD See Tofu.

BONITO The name given to several different fish, including a relative of mackerel (the Atlantic bonito) and another, a small tuna, the Pacific bonito. The latter is the fish used in Japanese cooking (known as *katsuo*): it is the strongest flavoured of the tuna and is used dried, in thin flakes known as *katsuo-bushi*. It is used to flavour stock and is sprinkled over dishes to season.

CHIKUWA See Fish Cakes.

DAIKON See Mooli.

ENOKI MUSHROOMS Small cultivated mushrooms with long thin stems and tiny white caps. They are harvested in clumps, attached at a root base which

Kamaboko and Chikuwa fish cakes

is cut off before use. They have a crisp texture and delicate flavour. They may be eaten raw or lightly cooked.

FISH CAKES These do not resemble the Western equivalent, they are finer and they are usually cooked ready for eating cold. Available fresh or frozen from Japanese supermarkets. *Chikuwa* are long, brown and white cakes; *kamaboko* is a smooth-textured white loaf; and *satsuma-age* are brown and come in many varieties.

GARI These pale pink ginger pickles are served with *Sushi* or *Sashimi* to refresh the palate between mouthfuls.

GINGER PICKLES Fresh root ginger is pickled in various strengths of flavour.

GOBO Burdock – a long, thin root

vegetable that grows wild in Europe, but is cultivated in Japan. The roots may be stored (unwashed) in a polythene bag in the fridge for up to two weeks. Scrub the roots, then cut into fine strips or grate them coarsely. The root may be soaked to remove bitter flavours and eaten raw, or cooked; it has a crisp raw texture and a slightly sweet and earthy flavour.

GOMA See Sesame Seeds.

HIJIKI A variety of dried seaweed. It is soaked, then used in soups and salads.

JAPANESE CURRY POWDER Available from Japanese supermarkets, this is essential for Japanese-style curries.

JAPANESE SPRING ONIONS Known as *negi*, these are larger than the European spring onions, with longer, thicker, blue-green stems.

KAMABOKO See Fish Cakes.

KATAKURI-KO Potato starch or flour. Cornflour can be used instead.

KATSUO-BUSHI See Bonito.

KOMBU Kelp seaweed, a rich source of iodine. Kombu is used to flavour stock and it is served as a vegetable. Dried kombu is dark grey-brown with a pale powdery covering which contributes to its flavour; therefore it is wiped, not washed, before use.

KONNYAKU A cake made from flour produced from a root vegetable called devil's tongue. It should be torn into pieces before cooking, rather than being cut with a knife, as this ensures it will absorb more flavour. Black and white varieties are available.

KOYA-TOFU Taking its name from Mount Koya, this is tofu which has been frozen. It was first used by the vegetarian Buddhist monks in the monastery on the mount when their tofu was frozen by the harsh winter snows. Freezing gives Koya-tofu a firmer texture with more resistance than ordinary tofu (slightly rubbery).

LOTUS ROOT The rhizome of a water lily. Fresh lotus roots (available from oriental supermarkets) are large with a red-brown skin which must be peeled off. They have a similar texture and

colour to potato, but the hollow channels running through them create an attractive flower pattern when sliced, making them a popular garnish. Canned lotus root is readily available.

MIRIN Sweet cooking sake, this has a delicate flavour and is usually added in the final stages of cooking.

MISO Fermented paste of soya beans, the key ingredient for miso soup and widely used as a seasoning. There are various types, depending on the culture used to ferment them which may be based on barley, wheat or soya bean starter mould. The time taken to mature the paste also affects the result. White miso has a lighter flavour than red miso; dark brown miso is a strong-flavoured version.

MOOLI Long white radish, also known as *daikon*. About the size of a parsnip (or larger) with smooth creamy-white skin, mooli has the crunchy texture and peppery flavour similar to red radishes but milder. It may be cooked (when it has a flavour reminiscent of turnip) or served raw in salads, grated for dips or as a garnish.

NEGI See Japanese Spring Onions.

NOODLES Various types are used. See Shirataki, Soba and Udon.

NORI Dried seaweed, sold in paper-thin sheets which are dark green to black in colour and almost transparent in places. It is toasted and used as a wrapping for sushi. Ready-toasted sheets (*yaki-nori*), seasoned with ingredients such as soy sauce, salt and sesame oil, are also readily available from healthfood shops.

OKONOMIYAKI SAUCE Similar to Tonkatsu Sauce, but sweeter.

PICKLES There are many varieties of pickled vegetables (*tsukemono*), served as accompaniments for rice dishes. Ask in your local supermarket for guidance on the types they stock. See also Gari and Umeboshi.

RICE VINEGAR This is a pale vinegar with a distinctive, delicate flavour. It is milder than most other light wine vinegars. It is available from healthfood shops and supermarkets as well as specialist stores. Do not confuse it with Chinese rice vinegar. The Mitsukan brand is widely available.

SAKE Japanese rice wine. Like Western wines, the price can vary. It is not necessary to use expensive sake for cooking. Sake is drunk hot or chilled.

SATSUMA-AGE See Fish Cakes.

SEAWEED Various types are used, dried or fresh. Seaweed is generally rich in minerals and vitamins, and can be a useful source of vegetable fibre. See Hijiki, Kombu, Nori and Wakame.

SESAME SEEDS Black or white, these are available roasted or plain. The plain seeds should be toasted before use.

SEVEN SPICE FLAVOUR OR PEPPER This chilli-based spice, known as *shichimi*, is made of hemp, poppy, rape and sesame seeds, anise-pepper leaves and tangerine peel.

SHICHIMI See Seven Spice Flavour.

SHIITAKE MUSHROOMS The most popular mushroom in Japan, this has a good flavour, especially when dried. Soaking water from dried shiitake makes a good stock.

SHIMEJI MUSHROOMS Similar to enoki mushrooms, these are separated into individual stems before using.

SHIRATAKI NOODLES White noodles made from the starch of the devil's tongue plant. Canned or packed in water, these are good for *Sukiyaki*.

SHIRATAMA-KO Rice flour made from glutinous short-grain rice with a high starch content. This is used to make *mochi* (sticky rice cakes).

SHISO LEAVES A Japanese herb similar to basil.

SHUNGIKU LEAVES Edible leaves of a Japanese chrysanthemum, these are good for *Sukiyaki*.

SOBA Long, thin buckwheat noodles. These are typically used in dishes from East Japan. Available from healthfood shops as well as Japanese supermarkets.

SOMEN Also known as soumen. Round white wheat flour noodles.

SOY SAUCE *Shoyu*, this is the best-known seasoning ingredient. There are several different types of Japanese soy sauce. Chinese soy sauce should not be substituted as it is far stronger. *Usukuchi soy sauce* is light in colour but has a saltier taste than dark soy sauce which is richer and stronger in flavour. It is good for boiling vegetables and for flavouring delicate dishes, such as clear soup. *Tamari* is a thick soy sauce with a mellow flavour. Used as a dip for *Sashimi* and other dishes. Regular soy sauce can be used instead.

SUSHI VINEGAR Seasoned and sweetened vinegar product for *Sushi*.

TAKUWAN A bright yellow, mooli pickle; a favourite with rolled *Sushi*.

TAMARI See Soy Sauce.

TOFU Also known as beancurd, this is a soya bean product valued for its high protein content in a vegetarian diet; it is also a good source of calcium and iron. There are several types, including soft or firm tofu; silken tofu; grilled *(yaki-tofu)*, fried or dried tofu; and *Koya-tofu* (see separate entry). Plain uncooked types are bland in themselves but readily absorb the flavour of other ingredients .

TONKATSU SAUCE Japanese fruity sauce served with deep-fried pork and croquettes.

UDON White ribbon noodles available fresh or dried. These are used in the cuisine of west Japan.

UMEBOSHI Small red pickled plums with a sharp and salty taste. Considered to act as a preservative, these are used as a filling for rice balls (*onigiri*).

USUKUCHI SOY SAUCE See Soy Sauce.

WAKAME Seaweed available fresh (vacuum packed) or dried, used for soups and salads.

WASABI Green horseradish which tastes extremely hot. Available as a paste or powdered, to which water is added (like making up mustard).

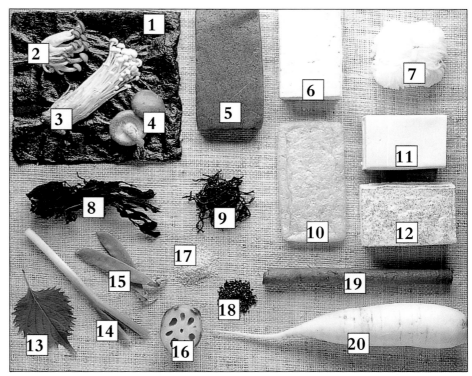

1 *Nori seaweed* 2 *Shimeji mushrooms* 3 *Enoki mushrooms* 4 *Shiitake mushrooms*
5 *Konnyaku* 6 *Fresh tofu* 7 *Shirataki noodles* 8 *Wakame seaweed* 9 *Hijiki seaweed*
10 *Fried tofu* 11 *Silken tofu* 12 *Grilled tofu* 13 *Shiso leaf* 14 *Japanese spring onions*
15 *Mangetouts* 16 *Lotus root* 17 *White sesame seeds* 18 *Black sesame seeds*
19 *Gobo* 20 *Mooli (daikon radish)*

FISH AND MEAT DISHES

From 1603 – 1867, Japan was still
very much an isolated country. During
this period, the government introduced a
policy of meat prohibition in order to
stop aggression in the population. As a
consequence, the Japanese concentrated
on fish and their knowledge of how to
prepare and cook fish became
unsurpassed. The fact that Japan is an
island gave the people access to a diverse
range of fresh fish, hence the custom of
eating the fish raw emerged.

After 1867, when Japan was opened
up to the world, meat was gradually
introduced into the diet. Previously
reserved for the sick, from this time
onwards meat was developed in
uniquely Japanese dishes.

Sliced Raw Salmon

Sliced fresh fish is known as *Sashimi*. This recipe introduces the cutting technique known as *hira zukuri*. Salmon is a good choice for those who have not tried sashimi before as most people are familiar with smoked salmon which is uncooked.

INGREDIENTS

Serves 4

2 fresh salmon fillets, skinned and any bones removed (about 400g/14oz total weight)

For the garnish

50g/2oz/¼ cup mooli (daikon radish)
wasabi paste
shiso leaf
soy sauce, to serve

1 Put the salmon fillets in a freezer for 10 minutes to make them easier to cut, then lay them skinned side up with the thick end to your right and away from you. Use a long sharp knife and tilt it to the left. Slice carefully towards you, starting the cut from the point of the knife, then slide the slice away from the fillet, to the right. Always slice from the far side towards you.

2 Finely shred the mooli, place in a bowl of cold water and leave for 5 minutes, then drain well.

3 Place three slices on a plate, then overlap another two slices on them diagonally. You can arrange fewer or more slices per portion, but an odd number looks better.

4 Garnish with the mooli, wasabi and shiso leaf, then serve immediately with a small bowl of soy sauce.

Brill Cured in Seaweed

The fish for this *Sashimi* is cut very fine by a technique called *sogi giri*, then flavoured with kombu. Begin a day in advance as the fish is cured overnight for this dish known as brill *Kobujime*. A small snapper, filleted, can be used instead of brill.

INGREDIENTS

Serves 4

200g/7oz brill fillets, skinned
4 sheets kombu seaweed (18 x 15cm/
   7 x 6in each)
165g/5½oz broccoli
salt

For the vinegar dressing

120ml/4fl oz/½ cup kombu and
   bonito stock
100ml/3½fl oz/generous ⅓ cup rice
   vinegar
30ml/2 tbsp soy sauce
7.5ml/1½ tsp sugar

1 Remove any stray bones from the brill and lay it skinned side up. Slice the fish into 4 x 4cm/1½ x 1½in pieces, as thin as a credit card, slicing the knife towards you, and sprinkle lightly with salt.

2 Clean the kombu seaweed by wiping it with a damp dish towel.

3 Lay the brill on a sheet of kombu in a single layer – do not pile up the slices. Then place another sheet of kombu on top. Repeat with the remaining kombu and brill.

4 Wrap tightly in clear film and place in a large shallow dish or tin. Put a book on top as a weight and place in the fridge overnight.

5 Cut the broccoli into small florets, discarding excess stems, then boil them until tender and drain. Refresh in cold water for 1 minute, then drain.

6 Place the ingredients for the vinegar dressing in a saucepan and bring to the boil. Remove the pan from the heat and leave the dressing to cool, then chill well. Discard the kombu wrapping from the brill.

7 Pile the brill into pyramid shapes in four small bowls or shallow plates. Place a small arrangement of broccoli on each portion and pour chilled sauce over just before serving the brill.

Poached Mackerel with Miso

This dish (*Mackerel Miso-ni*) is typical of Japanese-style mother's home cooking. There are many types of Japanese miso bean paste, including white miso which is sweet in flavour and dark miso which tastes salty. Darker miso is preferred for this recipe, but you can use any type.

INGREDIENTS

Serves 4

1 mackerel, gutted (675–750g/
    1¹/₂–1³/₄lb)
10g/¹/₄oz fresh root ginger, peeled and
    finely sliced
300ml/¹/₂ pint/1¹/₄ cups instant dashi
    (stock)
30ml/2 tbsp sugar
60ml/4 tbsp sake or dry white wine
115g/4oz/¹/₂ cup miso
10g/¹/₄oz fresh root ginger, peeled and
    finely shredded, to garnish

1 Chop the head off the mackerel and cut the fish into 2cm/³/₄in thick steaks. Soak the shredded ginger for the garnish in cold water for 5 minutes, then drain well.

— COOK'S TIP —

When boiling fish, lower it into boiling water. Do not cook from cold, otherwise the fish will smell unpleasant and the cooking liquid or soup will taste bitter.

2 Fold a sheet of foil just smaller than the diameter of a large shallow pan. Pour the stock, sugar and sake or wine into the pan. Bring to the boil, then arrange the mackerel in the pan in a single layer and add the sliced ginger. Spoon the soup over the mackerel and then place the foil over it. Simmer the mackerel for 5–6 minutes.

3 Dissolve the miso in a bowl in a little of the soup from the pan. Pour it back into the pan and simmer for a further 12 minutes, spooning the soup over the mackerel occasionally.

4 Use a draining spoon to remove the mackerel carefully from the pan and place on a plate. Spoon the remaining soup over and garnish with the shredded ginger, then serve hot.

Golden Marinated Mackerel

Marinating the mackerel gives it a delicious flavour and the same marinade is also good for pork. Deep fry the mackerel as soon as possible after coating it with cornflour.

INGREDIENTS

Serves 4
1 large mackerel, filleted
salt
oil, for deep frying
cornflour, for coating
$^1/_2$ bunch spring onions, shredded
   finely, to garnish

For the marinade
15g/$^1/_2$oz fresh root ginger
45ml/3 tbsp soy sauce
45ml/3 tbsp sake or dry white wine

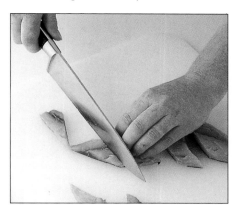

1 Remove any stray bones from the mackerel and cut it into 4cm/1$^1/_2$in long triangle-shaped pieces. Season the pieces with salt and set them aside for 5 minutes.

COOK'S TIP

Oil used for deep frying mackerel takes on the distinctive flavour of the fish and it is then unsuitable for other cooking, except, of course, when frying another batch of mackerel.

2 Grate the ginger and squeeze it to yield 7.5ml/1$^1/_2$ tsp ginger juice. Add the remaining marinade ingredients to the juice and mix well. Place the mackerel in the marinade and set aside for 30–60 minutes.

3 Soak the spring onions for the garnish in cold water for 5 minutes, then drain well.

4 Slowly heat the oil for deep frying to 170°C/340°F. Mop the pieces of mackerel well on paper towels, then dust them lightly with cornflour.

5 Deep fry the mackerel, turning the pieces until golden. Drain well and arrange on a plate. Sprinkle the spring onions on top and serve immediately.

Teriyaki Trout

Teriyaki sauce is very useful, not only for fish but also for meat.

INGREDIENTS

Serves 4
4 trout fillets

For the marinade
75ml/5 tbsp soy sauce
75ml/5 tbsp sake or dry white wine
75ml/5 tbsp mirin

COOK'S TIP

To make a teriyaki barbecue sauce, heat the marinade until boiling, then reduce it until it thickens. When you grill the fish or meat, brush it with the sauce several times.

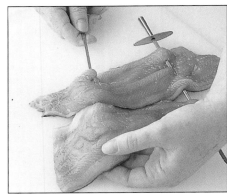

1 Lay the trout fillets in a shallow dish in a single layer. Mix the ingredients for the marinade and pour the marinade over the fish. Cover and marinate in the fridge for 5–6 hours, turning occasionally.

2 Thread two trout fillets neatly together on two metal skewers. Repeat with the remaining two fillets. You could cut the fillets in half if they are too big.

3 Grill the trout on a barbecue, over a high heat. Keep the fish about 10cm/4in away from the flame and brush it with the marinade several times. Grill each side until shiny and the trout is cooked through. Alternatively, cook the trout under a conventional grill.

4 Slide the trout off the skewers while it is hot. Serve hot or cold with any remaining marinade.

Grilled Tuna Kebabs

It is difficult to buy tuna fresh enough for *Sashimi*, so try this recipe. Choose a fatty portion of tuna steak. This oily, pinkish part of the tuna is better for grilling and has a good texture.

INGREDIENTS

Serves 4
200g/7oz tuna steak
bunch of spring onions
1 lime, quartered

For the marinade
10ml/2 tsp mirin
45ml/3 tbsp soy sauce

1 Cut the tuna into 24 cubes, each about 2cm/³/₄in. Mix the mirin and soy sauce, pour this over the tuna and leave to marinate for 30 minutes. Cut the spring onions into lengths, about 2.5cm/1in each.

COOK'S TIP

Soaking bamboo skewers in water for at least 30 minutes before using them helps to prevent them from catching fire under a hot grill or on the barbecue. Drain the skewers just before threading the food on them and cook the kebabs immediately after threading them.

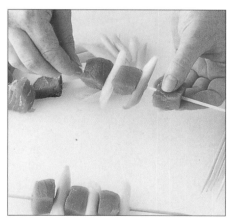

2 Thread the tuna and the spring onions alternately on to eight bamboo skewers.

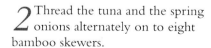

3 Preheat the grill to the hottest setting and grill the tuna, turning the skewers frequently to avoid burning them. Brush the tuna with the marinade several times during cooking. Grill until the tuna is lightly cooked but still moist inside.

4 Serve the kebabs immediately, with lime wedges.

Fried Swordfish

This is a light and tasty cold dish that is suitable for serving on a hot summer's day.

INGREDIENTS

Serves 4
4 swordfish steaks, boned, skin left on
  (about 600g/1lb 5oz total weight)
15ml/1 tbsp soy sauce
7.5ml/1½ tsp rice vinegar
bunch of spring onions
4 asparagus spears, trimmed
30ml/2 tbsp oil, for cooking

For the marinade
45ml/3 tbsp soy sauce
45ml/3 tbsp rice vinegar
30ml/2 tbsp sake or dry white wine
15ml/1 tbsp sugar
15ml/1 tbsp instant dashi (stock) or
  water
7.5ml/1½ tsp sesame oil

1 Cut the swordfish steaks into 4cm/1½in chunks and place in a dish. Pour the 15ml/1 tbsp soy sauce and 7.5ml/1½ tsp rice vinegar over the fish, then set aside for 5 minutes. Meanwhile, cut the spring onions into 3cm/1¼in lengths and the asparagus into 4cm/1½in lengths.

2 Mix the ingredients for the marinade in a dish. Heat three-quarters of the oil in a frying pan. Wipe the swordfish with paper towel and fry over a moderate heat for about 1–2 minutes on each side, or until cooked. Remove the fish from the frying pan and place it in the marinade.

3 Clean the frying pan and heat the remaining oil in it. Fry the spring onions over a moderate heat until browned, then add them to the fish. Fry the asparagus in the oil remaining in the pan over a low heat for 3–4 minutes, then add to the fish.

4 Leave the fish and vegetables to marinate for 10–20 minutes, turning the pieces occasionally. Serve the cold fish with the marinade on a large, deep plate.

Prawn and Avocado with Wasabi

This dish is a perfect starter for entertaining as it can be made easily; however, the whole dish must be made just before serving to prevent the avocado from discolouring and to preserve the flavour of the wasabi, which will be lost if allowed to stand for any length of time.

INGREDIENTS

Serves 4
2 avocados, halved, stoned and skinned
200g/7oz cooked king prawns, shelled,
  or 8 raw tiger prawns, heads removed

For the wasabi dressing
20ml/4 tsp usukuchi soy sauce
30ml/2 tbsp rice vinegar
10ml/2 tsp wasabi paste

1 Mix the ingredients for the wasabi dressing.

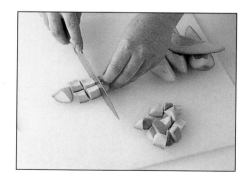

2 Cut each half of the avocados into 2cm/¾in cubes.

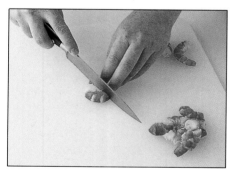

3 If using raw prawns, remove the black intestinal vein from the back with a toothpick. Cook them in salted simmering water for 1 minute, until they turn orange. Remove their shells and tails. Cut the prawns into pieces measuring about 2.5cm/1in long.

4 Put the prawns and the avocados in a bowl, and toss well with the dressing, then serve promptly.

Cod and Potato Croquettes

Croquettes are very popular in Japan and there are many kinds: these tasty fish croquettes are a perennial favourite.

INGREDIENTS

Serves 4
300g/11oz cod fillet
1 large mild onion, one-third sliced,
   the rest finely chopped
45ml/3 tbsp mayonnaise
400g/14oz potatoes, freshly boiled,
   peeled and coarsely mashed
plain flour, for shaping
1 egg, beaten
200g/7oz/3½ cups fresh white
   breadcrumbs
salt and white pepper
oil, for deep frying

For the garnish
1 lemon, cut into wedges
parsley sprigs

1 Lay the cod fillet on a large heatproof plate and sprinkle the sliced onion on top. Season with salt and white pepper. Cover with foil and stand the plate over a saucepan of simmering water. Cook for 15 minutes, or until the fish is opaque and flakes easily. Allow to cool.

2 Add the chopped onion, mayonnaise, 3ml/²⁄₃ tsp salt and white pepper to the warm potatoes. Mix well and allow to cool.

3 Discard the sliced onion, skin and bones from the fish. Put the fish in a plastic bag and pound it with a rolling pin until it is finely flaked.

4 Mix the cod into the potatoes. With floured hands, shape the mixture into eight oval, flat cakes. Press and mould the mixture firmly to press out any air as you shape the croquettes. Dip the croquettes in the beaten egg and coat them in the breadcrumbs. Chill for 30 minutes.

5 Heat the oil slowly to 180°C/350°F. Fry the croquettes in pairs to prevent them from bursting. Turn them in the oil, allowing about 3 minutes until crisp and golden. Drain well.

6 Place two croquettes on each plate. Garnish with lemon wedges and parsley and serve immediately.

Salmon Miso-Mayo

Mayonnaise goes well with miso in this tempting salmon dish, which is perfect for entertaining.

INGREDIENTS

Serves 4
4 portions salmon fillet (about 675g/1¹/₂lb total weight)
1 onion, thinly sliced
4 shiitake mushrooms, stems discarded and thinly sliced
30g/1¹/₄oz Cheddar cheese, grated

For the miso-mayo paste
120ml/8 tbsp mayonnaise
45ml/3 tbsp white or red miso

For the garnish
ground white sesame seeds
seven flavour spice (*shichimi*)(optional)

1 Preheat the oven to 180°C/ 350°F/Gas 4. Thoroughly mix the mayonnaise and the miso.

2 Make a deep cut in each of the salmon fillets without cutting through them completely.

— COOK'S TIP —

Make sure that the foil is large enough to seal well round the salmon. It is important not to lose any of the cooking juices from inside the parcel.

3 Cut four pieces of foil each large enough to completely enclose a portion of fish. Spread 22.5ml/1¹/₂ tbsp miso-mayo in the middle of each piece. Place a portion of salmon on the sauce, then divide the onion and mushrooms among the salmon pieces. Spoon the remaining miso-mayo and some of the grated cheese into the cuts in the salmon and top with the remaining grated cheese.

4 Sprinkle with ground white sesame seeds and seven flavour spice, if using, then enclose tightly in the foil. Bake for 10 minutes. Open the foil and bake for a further 5 minutes, until the cheese is lightly browned.

5 Serve immediately, transferring the open foil packets to plates.

Cod Poached in Foil

This way of cooking, in which the fish is steamed in a foil parcel, brings out the juices from the cod, which mingle with the flavours from the shiitake mushrooms, onions and sake to produce a delicious sauce.

INGREDIENTS

Serves 4

2 large cod fillets (about 600g/1lb 5oz total weight)
50g/2oz/4 tbsp butter or margarine, softened
1 large mild onion, thinly sliced
1 green pepper, seeded and sliced
4 shiitake mushrooms, stems discarded and sliced
30ml/2 tbsp sake or dry white wine
1 lemon, cut into wedges
20ml/4 tsp soy sauce
salt and white pepper

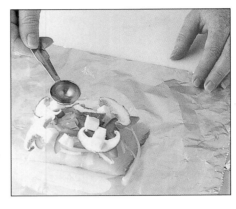

1 Halve each cod fillet and season with salt and white pepper. Cut four pieces of foil, each large enough to completely enclose a portion of cod.

2 Spread 5ml/1 tsp butter or margarine on each piece of foil and place the cod on top, dividing the onion, pepper and shiitake mushrooms between the four portions.

3 Top each with 10ml/2 tsp butter and sprinkle with 5ml/1 tsp sake or wine . Close the foil packets tightly so that steam cannot escape.

4 Place the packets in pairs in two frying pans or cook them in two batches. Pour in water carefully – do not pour it over the foil. Bring to the boil, cover closely, reduce the heat and simmer for 10 minutes. Top up the water if necessary.

5 Transfer the packets to plates and serve immediately, garnished with lemon wedges. Pour 5ml/1 tsp soy sauce over the contents of each packet just before eating the fish.

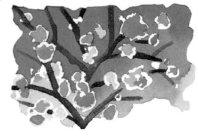

Prawn Tempura

Tempura is a delicate, delicious dish of savoury fritters in light batter. The secret for success is to use really cold water and to have the oil at the right temperature.

INGREDIENTS

Serves 4
8 raw tiger prawns, heads removed
oil, for deep frying
flour, for dusting

For the Tempura Dip
200ml/7fl oz/scant 1 cup water
45ml/3 tbsp mirin
10g/^{1}/$_4$oz bonito flakes
45ml/3 tbsp soy sauce

For the Tempura Batter
^{1}/$_2$ egg (see method)
90ml/6 tbsp iced water
75g/3oz/^{2}/$_3$ cup plain flour
2.5ml/^{1}/$_2$ tsp baking powder
2 ice cubes

For the garnish
65g/2^1/$_2$oz mooli (daikon radish), finely
  grated and drained
shiso leaf

1 Carefully shell the prawns, leaving their tails on. Cut a third of each tail off in a diagonal slit. Press out any excess water with your fingers to prevent it from seeping into the oil and spitting during cooking.

2 Make a shallow cut down the back of each prawn and remove the black intestinal vein.

3 Lay a prawn on its spine so that it is concave. Using a sharp knife, make three or four diagonal slits into the flesh, about two-thirds of the way in towards the spine, leaving all the pieces attached. Repeat with the remaining prawns: this keeps them straight during cooking. Flatten the prawns with your fingers.

4 To make the dip, put all the ingredients in a saucepan and bring to the boil. Remove from the heat, leave to cool and then strain.

5 Slowly heat the oil for deep frying to 185°C/365°F. Start making the batter when the oil is getting warm.

6 Always make the batter just before you use it so that it is still very cold. Stir, but do not beat, the egg in a large bowl and set aside half for another use. Add the iced water, flour and baking powder all at once. Stir only two or three times, leaving some free flour unblended and totally ignoring the lumps. Add the ice cubes.

7 Dust the prawns lightly with flour. Hold a prawn by the tail, quickly coat it with batter and slowly lower it into the oil. Do not drop the prawn into the oil as the coating comes off.

8 Repeat with the remaining prawns, frying them until they rise to the surface of the oil and are crisp. *Do not* fry until they are golden. Cook a few prawns at a time and then drain them well.

9 Pour the Tempura Dip into four small bowls. Place the tempura on a plate, garnish with the mooli and shiso leaf and serve immediately.

Crab Stick, Wakame and Cucumber Side Dish

In Japan, a couple of small side dishes are served with a main dish and this is a traditional recipe which harmonizes well within main courses.

INGREDIENTS

Serves 4

30g/1¼oz dried wakame seaweed
6 crab sticks
1 cucumber (about 200g/7oz)
5ml/1 tsp salt

For the vinegar dressing
22.5ml/4½ tsp sugar
2ml/⅓ tsp salt
100ml/3½fl oz/generous ⅓ cup rice
   vinegar
2.5ml/½ tsp usukuchi soy sauce

1 First make the vinegar dressing: dissolve the sugar and salt thoroughly in the vinegar, then stir in the soy sauce and chill.

2 Soak the dried wakame seaweed in warm water for 5 minutes. Meanwhile, shred the crab sticks.

3 Drain the wakame, cut it into 4cm/1½in long pieces and place in a dish. Cover and chill.

4 Cut the cucumber into 5mm/¼in slices – not too thin or too thick. Dissolve the 5ml/1 tsp salt in 200ml/7fl oz/scant 1 cup water and add the cucumber. Set aside for 5–6 minutes, but to preserve the flavour, do not soak it for any longer.

5 Drain the cucumber and dry it on a dish towel: wrap the towel around the cucumber and gently squeeze out the water. Then remove the cucumber from the towel, wrap it in clear film and chill.

6 When you are ready to serve the dish, mix the cucumber with the wakame and crab sticks, then add the dressing and toss the ingredients lightly together. Serve in four small bowls and pour 15ml/1 tbsp of the dressing over each portion of salad.

Fried Chicken

Chicken *Kara-age*, this is Japanese-style fried chicken flavoured with ginger. It makes a tasty snack or is equally delicious served as a main course. The chicken may be cooked with or without its skin, according to personal preference.

INGREDIENTS

Serves 4
8 boneless chicken thighs
oil, for deep frying
about 90g/3½oz/½ cup cornflour, for
   coating
salad leaves, to garnish

For the marinade
50g/2oz fresh root ginger
60ml/4 tbsp sake or dry white wine
60ml/4 tbsp soy sauce

1 Grate the ginger and squeeze it over a bowl to extract its juice. Add the sake or wine and soy sauce. Cut the chicken thighs into four chunks and rub well with the marinade, then set aside in the marinade for 30 minutes.

2 Heat the oil slowly to 165–170°C/ 330–340°F. Pat the chicken dry on paper towel. When the oil is hot, dust the chicken generously with cornflour and lower the pieces into the oil. To maintain the oil temperature, do not add too many chicken pieces at once. Deep fry the chicken pieces for 4–5 minutes, until crisp, golden and cooked through.

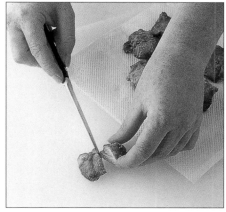

3 Halve one chicken piece to make sure it is cooked inside. Drain the rest of the chicken, then serve hot or cold, garnished with salad leaves.

Yakitori Chicken

Yakitori are Japanese-style chicken kebabs. They are easy to eat and ideal for barbecues or parties.

INGREDIENTS

Serves 4
6 boneless chicken thighs (with skin)
bunch of spring onions
seven flavour spice (*shichimi*), to serve (optional)

For the yakitori sauce
150ml/¼ pint/⅔ cup soy sauce
90g/3½oz/½ cup sugar
25ml/5 tsp sake or dry white wine
15ml/1 tbsp plain flour

1 To make the sauce, stir the soy sauce, sugar and sake or wine into the flour in a small saucepan and bring to the boil, stirring. Reduce the heat and simmer for 10 minutes, until the sauce is reduced by one-third. Then set aside.

2 Cut each chicken thigh into six chunks and cut the spring onions into 3cm/1¼in long pieces.

3 Thread the chicken and spring onions alternately on to 12 bamboo skewers. Grill under a medium heat or on the barbecue, brushing generously several times with the sauce. Allow 5–10 minutes, until the chicken is cooked but still moist.

4 Serve with a little extra yakitori sauce, offering seven flavour spice with the kebabs if possible.

Chicken Cakes with Teriyaki Sauce

These small chicken cakes, about the size of small meatballs, are known as *Tsukune*. Here, they are cooked with a glaze and garnished with spring onions.

INGREDIENTS

Serves 4
For the chicken cakes
400g/14oz minced chicken
1 size 4 egg
60ml/4 tbsp grated onion
7.5ml/1½ tsp sugar
7.5ml/1½ tsp soy sauce
cornflour, for coating
15ml/1 tbsp oil
½ bunch spring onions, finely shredded, to garnish

For the teriyaki sauce
30ml/2 tbsp sake or dry white wine
30ml/2 tbsp sugar
30ml/2 tbsp mirin
30ml/2 tbsp soy sauce

1 Mix the minced chicken with the egg, grated onion, sugar and soy sauce until the ingredients are thoroughly combined and well bound together. This process takes about 3 minutes, until the mixture is quite sticky, which gives a good texture. Shape the mixture into 12 small, flat round cakes and dust them lightly all over with cornflour.

2 Soak the spring onions in cold water for 5 minutes and drain well.

3 Heat the oil in a frying pan. Place the chicken cakes in the pan in a single layer, and cook over a moderate heat for 3 minutes. Turn the cakes and cook for 3 minutes on the second side.

4 Mix the ingredients for the sauce and pour it into the pan. Turn the chicken cakes occasionally until they are evenly glazed. Move or gently shake the pan constantly to prevent the sauce from burning.

5 Arrange the chicken cakes on a plate and top with the spring onions. Serve immediately.

COOK'S TIP

To make *Tsukune Chicken*, a grilled version of this recipe, make smaller chicken cakes. Cook them under a moderately hot grill, brushing with the Teriyaki Sauce.

Vegetable-stuffed Beef Rolls

Thinly sliced meats are used almost daily in Japanese cooking, so there are countless recipes for them. These stuffed beef rolls, or *Yahata-maki*, are very popular for picnic meals. You can roll up other vegetables in the beef, for example asparagus tips; pork is also good cooked this way.

INGREDIENTS

Serves 4
50g/2oz carrot
50g/2oz green pepper, seeded
bunch of spring onions
400g/14oz beef topside, thinly sliced
plain flour, for dusting
15ml/1 tbsp oil
parsley sprigs, to garnish

For the sauce
30ml/2 tbsp sugar
45ml/3 tbsp soy sauce
45ml/3 tbsp mirin

1 Shred the carrot and green pepper into 4–5cm/1½–2in lengths. Halve the spring onions lengthways, then shred them diagonally into 4–5cm/1½–2in lengths.

2 The beef slices should be 2mm/½in thick, no thicker, and about 15cm/6in square. Lay a slice of beef on a board and top with carrot, green pepper and spring onion strips. Roll up quite tightly and dust lightly with flour. Repeat with the remaining beef and vegetables.

3 Heat the oil in a frying pan. Add the beef rolls, placing the joins underneath to prevent them from unrolling. Fry over a moderate heat until golden and cooked, turning occasionally.

4 Add the ingredients for the sauce and increase the heat. Roll the beef quickly to glaze the rolls.

5 Remove the rolls from the pan and halve them, cutting at a slant. Stand the rolls, with the sloping cut end facing upwards on a plate. Dress with the sauce and garnish with parsley. Serve hot or cold.

Japanese-style Hamburgers

This recipe makes soft and moist hamburgers that are delicious with rice, especially with the mooli topping which adds its own refreshing flavour.

INGREDIENTS

Serves 4

30ml/2 tbsp oil, plus extra for greasing hands
1 small onion, finely chopped
500g/1¼lb minced beef
50g/2oz/1 cup fresh white breadcrumbs
1 egg
5ml/1 tsp salt
black pepper
115g/4oz shiitake mushrooms, stems discarded and sliced
200g/7oz mooli (daikon radish), finely grated and drained in a sieve
4 shiso leaves, finely shredded (optional)
30ml/1½ tbsp soy sauce

1 Heat 15ml/1 tbsp oil in a frying pan and fry the onion gently until soft but not browned. Leave to cool.

2 Put the minced beef in a large bowl with the fried onion, breadcrumbs and egg. Season with the salt and pepper. Knead well by hand until the ingredients are thoroughly combined and the mixture becomes sticky. It is important to keep the meat soft and juicy for this recipe. Divide the mixture into four.

3 Put a little oil on your hands. Take a portion of the mixture and throw it from one hand to the other five or six times to remove any air. Then shape the mixture into a 2cm/¾in thick burger. Repeat with the remaining mixture.

4 Heat the remaining oil in a frying pan and add the burgers. Fry over a high heat until browned on one side, then turn over. Place the shiitake mushrooms in the pan, next to the burgers, cover and cook over a low heat for 3–4 minutes or until cooked through, stirring the mushrooms occasionally.

5 Serve the burgers topped with the mooli, shiitake mushrooms and shiso leaves (if used). Pour 7.5ml/1½ tsp soy sauce over each burger just before it is served.

Simmered Beef with Potatoes

Another typical example of Japanese home cooking, known as *Nikujaga*, this would be thought of as one of mother's special dishes.

INGREDIENTS

Serves 4
4 medium potatoes, peeled
300g/11oz beef topside, thinly sliced
30ml/2 tbsp frozen peas
15ml/1 tbsp oil
1 large mild onion, cut into wedges
200ml/7fl oz/scant 1 cup instant dashi (stock) or water
30ml/2 tbsp sugar
22.5ml/4½ tsp sake or dry white wine
22.5ml/4½ tsp mirin
22.5ml/4½ tsp soy sauce

1 Cut each potato into thirds or quarters and soak them in cold water for 5 minutes. Drain well.

2 Cut the beef into 3–4cm/ 1¼–1½in long strips. Pour hot water over the frozen peas and leave until thawed, then drain.

3 Heat the oil in a deep frying pan or saucepan. Remove from the heat and add the beef. Replace the pan on the heat and fry the beef for 1 minute. Add the onion and potatoes, and fry for a further 2 minutes.

4 Fold a sheet of foil in half so that it is just smaller than the diameter of the frying pan. Pour in the stock or water and bring to the boil. Skim the broth carefully. When the soup clears, cover the pan with the foil and simmer for 3–4 minutes. Stir in the sugar and sake or wine, cover and simmer for a further 4–5 minutes.

5 Add the mirin and 15ml/3 tsp soy sauce, re-cover the pan and simmer for 6–7 minutes.

6 Finally, stir in the remaining soy sauce and simmer, uncovered, until only a little soup remains. Shake the pan gently occasionally to prevent the ingredients from burning. Serve the beef and potatoes in a large bowl, sprinkled with the peas.

Pork and Beef Cabbage Rolls

INGREDIENTS

Serves 4

16 soft green cabbage leaves
150g/5oz lean minced pork
150g/5oz lean minced beef
1 small onion, finely chopped
2.5ml/¹/₂ tsp salt, plus extra for
   seasoning
black pepper
115g/4oz boiled Japanese rice
punnet of cress
prepared English mustard or Japanese
   karashi mustard, to serve

For the soup

1.2 litres/2 pints/5 cups instant dashi
   (stock)
30ml/2 tbsp sake or dry white wine
30ml/2 tbsp mirin
30ml/2 tbsp soy sauce

1 Boil the cabbage leaves for 1–2 minutes, drain well and leave to cool. To flatten the leaves, carefully slice out the thick vein, chop it finely and place it in a bowl.

2 Add the pork and beef to the chopped cabbage and mix in the onion. Season lightly with salt and pepper and add the rice. Knead the mixture thoroughly by hand until the ingredients are combined and the mixture binds well. Divide the mixture into eight portions.

3 Overlap two cabbage leaves flat and place a portion of mixture on top in a thick cylinder shape. Wrap the leaves carefully around the meat, then close the roll neatly with a wooden cocktail stick. Make eight cabbage rolls.

4 Cut the cress off its roots, wash and drain it.

5 Bring the ingredients for the soup to the boil in a large saucepan, adding the 2.5ml/¹/₂ tsp salt. Then reduce the heat so that it simmers steadily. Add the cabbage rolls and cover the pan. Simmer gently for 40 minutes. Just before removing the pan from the heat, add the cress to the soup.

6 Slice each cabbage roll into three or four pieces, removing the cocktail sticks, and arrange them on deep plates or a single serving dish. Pour the soup over and serve immediately, with prepared English or karashi mustard.

Fried Pork in a Ginger Marinade

Ginger – *shoga* – is a popular spice in Japanese cooking. Plain cooked rice complements this recipe very well.

INGREDIENTS

Serves 4

400g/14oz pork loin, cut into slices
   1cm/½ in thick
2 tomatoes
punnet of cress
mixed salad leaves, for serving
7.5ml/1½ tsp oil, for cooking

For the marinade

20g/¾oz fresh root ginger
60ml/4 tbsp soy sauce
15ml/1 tbsp sake or dry white wine

1 To prepare the marinade, grate the ginger and squeeze it well over a dish to yield 5ml/1 tsp ginger juice. Mix in the soy sauce and sake or wine. Place the pork slices in a shallow dish, pour over the marinade and turn them to coat well. Set aside for about 15 minutes.

2 Meanwhile cut the tomatoes into four wedges. Cut the cress off its roots, wash and drain it. Chill the prepared ingredients and salad leaves.

3 Heat the oil in a frying pan. Place the pork in the pan, in a single layer and add the marinade. Fry over a medium-high heat, turning the pork once, until golden on both sides.

4 Arrange the pork on a plate with the salad leaves, tomatoes and cress. Pour cooking juices from the pan over the pork and serve immediately.

Deep Fried Pork Strips with Shredded Cabbage

Deep-fried pork is very tasty when served with soft green cabbage and a fruity sauce, known as *Tonkatsu*. This dish is enjoyed throughout Japan.

INGREDIENTS

Serves 4
4 boneless pork loin steaks (115g/4oz each)
7.5ml/1¹⁄₂ tsp salt
black pepper
plain flour, for coating
2 eggs, very lightly beaten
50g/2oz fresh white breadcrumbs
¹⁄₂ soft green cabbage, finely shredded
oil, for deep frying

For the sauce
100ml/3¹⁄₂fl oz/generous ¹⁄₃ cup brown sauce (select a fruity brand)
45ml/3 tbsp tomato ketchup
15ml/1 tbsp sugar

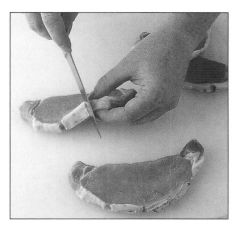

1 Snip any fat on the pork steaks to ensure the meat remains flat when frying. Then beat the pork with a meat mallet or rolling pin to tenderize it. Season with the salt and black pepper, and dust the pork lightly with flour.

--- COOK'S TIP ---

Commercial Japanese *Tonkatsu* sauce is available ready prepared and it may be substituted for the ingredients given above.

2 Dip the steaks into the egg first and then coat them with the breadcrumbs. Press the breadcrumbs on to the steaks with your fingers to ensure they stick well. Chill for about 10 minutes to allow the coating time to set slightly.

3 Meanwhile, soak the shredded cabbage in cold water for about 5 minutes. Drain well and chill. Mix the ingredients for the sauce, stirring until the sugar has dissolved.

4 Slowly heat the oil for deep frying to 165–170°C/330–340°F. Deep fry two steaks at a time for about 6 minutes, turning them until they are crisp and golden. Skim any floating breadcrumbs from the oil occasionally to prevent them from burning. Drain the steaks well and keep hot.

5 Cut the steaks into 2cm/³⁄₄in strips and place on a plate. Arrange the cabbage beside the pork and pour the sauce over. Serve immediately.

VEGETABLE, EGG AND TOFU DISHES

Recipes for these basic foods were developed by the Japanese as a response to the lack of meat in the diet. Many vegetables are unique to Japan, such as wakame and hijiki seaweed, which are both nutritious and healthy.

Eggs, too, were considered important as they are full of protein. However, they were expensive and so were mixed with stocks to make them go further.

Tofu was introduced from China. High in protein and low in fat, it readily absorbs the flavours of the dish in which it is used. It is ideal for vegetarians as an alternative to meat and can be eaten raw, deep fried or steamed.

Spinach with Bonito Flakes

This is a cold side dish of lightly cooked spinach dressed with fine bonito flakes. A similar vegetarian side dish can be prepared by omitting the bonito flakes and marinating the spinach in kombu seaweed stock and the soy sauce.

INGREDIENTS

Serves 4
300g/11oz whole spinach, roots trimmed

For the marinade
60ml/4 tbsp kombu and bonito stock or instant dashi
20ml/4 tsp usukuchi soy sauce
60ml/4 tbsp fine bonito flakes (*katsuobushi*)

1 Wash the spinach thoroughly. Keep the stems together, then hold the leaves of the spinach and lower the stems into boiling water for 10 seconds before lowering the leaves into the water and boiling for 1–2 minutes. Do not overcook the spinach.

2 Meanwhile, prepare a large bowl of cold water. Drain the spinach and soak it in the cold water for 1 minute to preserve its colour and remove any bitterness.

3 Drain the spinach and squeeze it well, holding the stems upwards and squeezing firmly down the length of the leaves.

4 Mix the stock and soy sauce in a dish and marinate the spinach in this mixture for 10–15 minutes, turning it over once.

5 Squeeze the spinach lightly and cut it into 3–4cm/1¼ –1½in long pieces, reserving the marinade. Divide the spinach between four small bowls, arranging the pieces so that the cut edges face upwards. Sprinkle 15ml/1 tbsp bonito flakes and a little of the marinade over each portion, then serve immediately.

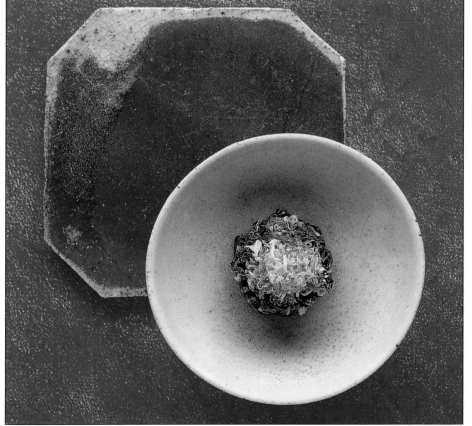

French Beans with Sesame Seeds

When made with kombu seaweed stock, this is an excellent vegetarian dish which can be served as a starter or as an accompaniment to a main course. The sauce, made from sesame seeds (*goma*), also tastes very good with other vegetables, such as carrots.

INGREDIENTS

Serves 4
200g/7oz French beans
salt

For the gomaae sauce
60ml/4 tbsp white sesame seeds
10ml/2 tsp sugar
15ml/1 tbsp soy sauce
15ml/1 tbsp instant dashi (stock)

1 Trim both ends off the French beans. Cook the French beans in boiling salted water for 2 minutes, until they are tender. Prepare a large bowl of cold water.

2 Drain the cooked beans and soak them in the cold water for 1 minute to preserve their colour. Drain well and cut into 3–4cm/1¼–1½in long pieces. Chill for 5 minutes.

3 Meanwhile make the gomaae sauce. Grind the sesame seeds in a mortar, using a pestle, leaving some of the sesame seeds whole. If you do not have a pestle and mortar, roughly chop the sesame seeds on a chopping board with a knife.

4 Stir in the sugar, then add the soy sauce and stock, and mix well with a rubber spatula.

5 To serve, put the chilled beans in a bowl, add the sauce and toss well. Transfer the beans to four small bowls, and serve immediately.

Japanese-style Potato Salad

The potatoes are stir-fried with carrots and onion, then cooked in stock before egg is added.

INGREDIENTS

Serves 4

4 medium potatoes
2 carrots
1 large mild onion
20ml/4 tsp oil
1 vegetable stock cube
20ml/4 tsp rice vinegar
10ml/2 tsp sugar
2.5ml/½ tsp salt, plus extra for
    cucumber
2 size 4 eggs, beaten
½ cucumber

1 Cut the potatoes lengthways into four, then slice the pieces across into thick chunks. Soak the potatoes in cold water for 2 minutes and drain well.

2 Halve the carrots vertically, then slice them across into chunks. Cut the onion into thick wedges.

3 Heat the oil in a deep frying pan or saucepan. Stir-fry the potatoes, carrots and onion for 1 minute. Dissolve the vegetable stock cube in 200ml/7fl oz/scant 1 cup boiling water and pour it into the pan. Add the rice vinegar, sugar and salt. Cover and simmer for 5 minutes. Uncover and cook over a moderate heat until all the liquid has evaporated. Shake the pan gently occasionally to prevent the vegetables from sticking to the pan as the liquid dries up.

4 Remove from the heat and allow to cool for 30 seconds, then add the beaten egg stirring quickly until the egg sets. Transfer to a dish and leave to cool, then chill.

5 Meanwhile halve the cucumber vertically and cut it into thin slices. Place the cucumber in a colander or sieve over a bowl. Sprinkle with a little salt and leave to stand for 10 minutes. Gently squeeze out the liquid from the cucumber.

6 Add the cucumber to the potato mixture and check the seasoning, adding more salt, if necessary. Serve chilled.

Seaweed Salad with Broad Beans

INGREDIENTS

Serves 4

25g/1oz dried wakame seaweed
115g/4oz onion, thinly sliced
1 fresh red chilli, or 1 dried, soaked in
    cold water for 5 minutes
200g/7oz/1½ cups fresh shelled broad
    beans
salt

For the marinade
5ml/1 tsp soy sauce
5ml/1 tsp rice vinegar

For the dressing
37.5ml/7½ tsp instant dashi (stock)
37.5ml/7½ tsp rice vinegar
2ml/⅓ tsp salt
7.5ml/1½ tsp soy sauce

1 Soak the seaweed in cold water for 10 minutes, then cut it into 3–4cm/1¼ –1½in strips. Soak the onion in cold water for 10 minutes.

2 Finely slice the chilli, discarding the seeds, if preferred. Cook the broad beans in boiling salted water until tender, then drain them and remove their skins.

3 Mix the seaweed, drained onions and broad beans in a shallow dish. Mix the marinade ingredients and pour it over the salad, then chill until ready to serve, or for at least 1 hour.

4 Mix the ingredients for the dressing and chill it separately from the salad. Pour the dressing over the vegetables just before serving the salad, topped with the chilli. Serve chilled.

COOK'S TIP

Young broad beans are best for this salad. They take about 5 minutes to cook. Larger or older beans require 7–10 minutes cooking.

Mooli with Sesame Miso Sauce

This simple vegetable dish makes a good starter for a dinner party.

INGREDIENTS

Serves 4
1 medium mooli (daikon radish), about 800g/1³/₄lb
15ml/1 tbsp rice, washed
1 sheet kombu seaweed (20 x 10cm/ 8 x 4in)
punnet of cress, to garnish
salt

For the sesame miso sauce
75g/3oz/generous ¹/₃ cup red miso paste
75g/3oz/generous ¹/₃ cup white miso paste
60ml/4 tbsp mirin
30ml/2 tbsp sugar
20ml/4 tsp ground white sesame seeds

1 Slice the mooli into 2cm/³/₄in thick slices, then peel off the skin. Wrap the rice in a piece of muslin or cheesecloth and tie it with string, allowing room for the rice to expand during cooking. The bundle of rice should look like a commercial dried bouquet garni.

2 Place the mooli in a saucepan and fill with water. Add the rice bag and a little salt, bring to the boil, then simmer for 15 minutes. Gently drain the mooli and discard the rice.

COOK'S TIP
The small bag of uncooked rice is added to the cooking water to keep the mooli white during cooking and remove any bitterness from the vegetable.

3 Place the seaweed in a large shallow pan, lay the mooli on top and fill with water. Bring to the boil, then simmer for 20 minutes.

4 Meanwhile, make the sauce. Mix the red and white miso pastes well in a saucepan. Add the mirin and sugar, then simmer for 5–6 minutes, stirring continuously. Remove from the heat and add the sesame seeds.

5 Arrange the mooli and seaweed in a large dish with their hot cooking stock. Sprinkle cress over the top. Serve the mooli on small plates with the sesame miso sauce poured over and garnished with some of the cress. The seaweed is used only to flavour the mooli, it is not eaten.

Spicy Fried Celery

This is a simple, spicy side dish which complements meat or vegetable main courses alike. To enjoy this dish at its best, it is very important to avoid overcooking the vegetables as they should be crisp.

INGREDIENTS

Serves 4

4 celery sticks with some leaves
1 dried red chilli, soaked in cold water for 5 minutes
15ml/1 tbsp oil
20ml/4 tsp sugar
30ml/2 tbsp soy sauce

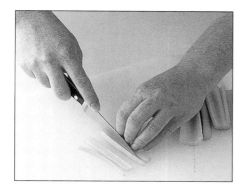

1 Cut the celery leaves in pieces measuring about 2.5cm/1in long. Cut the celery sticks into 4cm/1¹/₂in lengths, then finely shred these vertically.

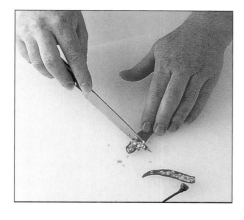

2 Cut the stalk off the chilli, then cut it in half lengthways. Scrape out the seeds. Thinly slice the flesh.

3 Heat the oil in a frying pan and add the chilli, celery and sugar. Stir-fry over a moderate heat for 1 minute, then add the soy sauce and continue stir-frying for a further 1 minute.

4 Add the celery leaves and stir-fry until all the cooking liquor from the ingredients has evaporated. To keep the celery crisp, evaporate the liquid quickly.

5 Serve the celery in four small bowls and garnish with the chilli slices.

Rolled Omelette

This is a firmly set, rolled omelette, which is cut into neat pieces and can be served hot or cold. The texture should be smooth and soft, not leathery, and the flavour is sweet-savoury. Mooli and soy sauce are perfect condiments to complement its flavour and texture.

INGREDIENTS

Serves 4
8 eggs
60ml/4 tbsp sugar
20ml/4 tsp soy sauce
90ml/6 tbsp sake or dry white wine
vegetable oil, for cooking

For the garnish

8cm/3¼in length of mooli (daikon radish), finely grated
shiso leaves
gari (ginger pickles)
soy sauce, to serve

1 Break the eggs into a large bowl. Do not beat the eggs, but mix them together by stirring using a pair of chopsticks and a cutting action.

2 Mix the sugar with the soy sauce and sake or wine in a small bowl. Lightly stir this mixture into the eggs. Pour half the mixture into another bowl as it will be cooked in two equal batches.

3 Heat a little oil in a frying pan and wipe off the excess.

4 Pour a quarter of the mixture from one bowl into the pan, tilting the pan to coat it with a thin layer. When the edge has set, but the middle is moist, roll up the egg towards you.

5 Moisten a paper towel with oil and grease the empty side of the pan. Pour a third of the remaining egg into the pan. Lift the rolled egg up with your chopsticks and let the raw egg run underneath it.

6 When the edge has set, roll up the omelette in the opposite direction, tilting the pan away from you so that the egg rolls easily.

7 Slide the roll towards you again, grease the pan and pour half of the remaining mixture on to it, allowing the egg to run under the roll as before. When set, insert the chopsticks in the side of the rolled omelette, then flip it over towards the opposite side of the pan. Cook the remaining egg in the same way.

8 Slide the roll so that its join is underneath. Cook for 10 seconds.

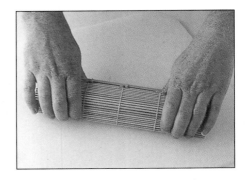

9 Slide the roll out on to a bamboo mat and roll up tightly, then press neatly into a rectangular shape. Leave to cool. Cook the second batch of egg mixture in the same way. Slice the cold omelettes into 2.5cm/1in thick pieces and garnish with mooli, shiso and gari. Serve with soy sauce.

Rice Omelette

Rice omelettes are a great favourite with Japanese children, who usually top them with tomato ketchup.

INGREDIENTS

Serves 4

115g/4oz skinned boneless chicken thigh, cut into 1cm/¹/₂in cubes
35ml/7 tsp butter
1 small onion, chopped
30g/1¹/₄oz/¹/₄ cup carrot, chopped
2 shiitake or closed cup mushrooms, stems removed and chopped
15ml/1 tbsp finely chopped parsley
380g/13 oz/2¹/₄ cups freshly boiled rice
30ml/2 tbsp tomato ketchup
6 size 1 eggs
60ml/4 tbsp milk
3ml/²/₃ tsp salt plus extra to season and black or white pepper

For the garnish
tomato ketchup
parsley sprigs

1 Season the chicken with salt and pepper. Melt 7.5ml/1¹/₂ tsp butter in a frying pan. Fry the onion for 1 minute, then add the chicken and fry until the chicken is white and cooked. Add the carrots and mushrooms, stir-fry until soft over a moderate heat, then add the parsley. Set this mixture aside and clean the frying pan.

2 Melt 7.5ml/1¹/₂ tsp butter in the frying pan, add the rice and stir well. Mix in the fried ingredients, tomato ketchup and pepper. Stir well, adding salt to taste if necessary. Keep the mixture warm.

3 Beat the eggs lightly, add the milk, 3ml/²/₃ tsp salt and pepper.

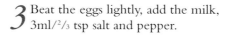

4 Melt 5ml/1 tsp butter in an omelette pan over a moderate heat. Pour in a quarter of the egg mixture and stir it briefly with a fork, then leave to set for 1 minute. Top with a quarter of the rice mixture.

5 Fold the omelette over the rice and slide it to the edge of the pan to shape it into a curve. Do not cook the omelette too much.

6 Invert the omelette on to a warmed plate, cover with a paper towel and press neatly into a rectangular shape. Cook another three omelettes from the remaining ingredients. Serve immediately with tomato ketchup on top, garnished with parsley.

Salmon Sealed with Egg

Tamago-toji, meaning egg cover, is the Japanese title for this type of dish which can be made from various ingredients. Canned pink salmon is used here for a very delicate flavour. Fried beancurd can be used instead of salmon.

INGREDIENTS

Serves 4
1 x 400g/14oz can pink salmon, drained, bones and skin removed
10 mangetouts, trimmed
2 large mild onions, sliced
40ml/8 tsp sugar
30ml/2 tbsp soy sauce
4 size 4 eggs, beaten

1 Flake the salmon. Boil the mange-touts for 2–3 minutes, drain and slice finely.

2 Put the onions in a frying pan, add 200ml/7fl oz/scant 1 cup water and bring to the boil. Cook for 5 minutes over a moderate heat, then add the sugar and soy sauce. Cook for a further 5 minutes.

3 Add the salmon and cook for 2–3 minutes or until the soup has virtually evaporated. Pour the egg over to cover the surface. Sprinkle in the mangetouts and cover the pan. Cook for 1 minute over a moderate heat, until just set. Do not overcook or the eggs will curdle and separate. Spoon on to a plate from the pan and serve immediately.

Japanese Savoury Custard

INGREDIENTS

Serves 4
3 size 3 eggs
3ml/²⁄₃ tsp salt
5ml/1 tsp usukuchi soy sauce
3ml/²⁄₃ tsp sugar
400ml/14fl oz/1²⁄₃ cups kombu and bonito stock
50g/2oz chicken breast fillet, thinly sliced
4 shiitake mushrooms, stems removed and sliced
4 medium prawns, shelled and thawed if frozen
10ml/2 tsp sake or dry white wine
10ml/2 tsp soy sauce
mitsuba leaves or cress to garnish

1 Break the eggs into a bowl. To avoid introducing too much air, do not beat the eggs, but stir them using a pair of chopsticks and a cutting action.

2 Stir the salt, usukuchi soy sauce and sugar into the cold stock, then add the egg. Strain the mixture through a fine sieve into another bowl.

3 Season the chicken, shiitake mushrooms and prawns with the sake or wine and soy sauce, then divide them equally between four custard cups or individual soufflé dishes. Pour the egg mixture over.

4 Place in a steamer over a saucepan or wok of boiling water and cover. Steam over a medium-high heat for 2–3 minutes, then remove the lid from the steamer and lay a dish towel over the top. Replace the lid and cook over a low heat for 18–20 minutes, or until set.

5 Insert a bamboo skewer to check if the mixture is cooked: if a little clear liquid comes out, it is cooked. Garnish with mitsuba leaves or cress. If you have lids for the cups, put them on and serve immediately. Provide spoons with which to eat the custard.

Scrambled Tofu with Spring Onions

This is a tasty dish which may be served as a side dish or as a nutritious vegetarian main dish. Serve rice as an accompaniment.

INGREDIENTS

Serves 4

1 packet of fresh Japanese tofu (10 x 8 x 3cm/4 x 3¼ x 1¼in), 300g/11oz weighed without water
6 spring onions
45ml/3 tbsp butter
1 egg

For the seasoning

15ml/1 tbsp sake or dry white wine
15ml/1 tbsp sugar
15ml/1 tbsp soy sauce
5ml/1 tsp salt

1 Wrap the tofu in a dish towel and place it on a chopping board. Put a large plate on top and leave for about 30 minutes to remove any excess water. Then coarsely crush the tofu by hand.

2 Thinly slice the green part of two spring onions and finely chop the remainder of the onions.

3 Melt the butter in a saucepan and add the tofu. Break up the tofu well with a spatula, add all the seasoning ingredients and stir-fry for 2–3 minutes. Add the chopped spring onions and keep stirring until all the cooking juices have evaporated.

4 Lightly beat the egg and pour it over the tofu. Mix it in quickly. When the egg has set, add the green part of the spring onions and stir well.

5 Serve in four small bowls, hot or at room temperature.

Tofu Steaks

Vegetarians and those who eat meat will equally enjoy these tasty tofu steaks.

INGREDIENTS

Serves 4

1 packet of fresh Japanese tofu (10 x 8 x 3cm/4 x 3¼ x 1¼in), 300g/11oz weighed without water
30ml/2 tbsp oil

For the marinade

45ml/3 tbsp sake
30ml/2 tbsp usukuchi soy sauce
5ml/1 tsp sesame oil
1 garlic clove, crushed
15ml/1 tbsp grated fresh root ginger
1 spring onion, finely chopped

For the garnish

2 spring onions, thinly sliced
mixed salad leaves
seven flavour spice (*shichimi*), to serve

1 Wrap the tofu in a dish towel and place it on a chopping board. Put a large plate on top and leave the tofu for 30 minutes to remove any excess water.

2 Slice the tofu horizontally into three pieces, then cut the slices into quarters. Thoroughly mix the ingredients for the marinade in a large dish. Add the tofu in a single layer and set aside for 30 minutes.

3 Heat half the oil in a frying pan and cook half the tofu steaks. Fry over a moderate heat for 3 minutes on each side, or until golden. Repeat.

4 Arrange three tofu steaks on each plate. Heat any remaining marinade and it may be poured over the steaks. Sprinkle with the spring onions and garnish with mixed salad leaves. Serve immediately with seven flavour spice if available.

Boiled Fried Beancurd with Hijiki Seaweed

Boiled dishes, known as *Nimono*, are enjoyed throughout the year.

Ingredients

Serves 4

20g/³⁄₄oz dried hijiki seaweed
1 sheet Japanese fried beancurd
30g/1¼oz carrots
30g/1¼oz fresh shiitake mushrooms, stems removed
15ml/1 tbsp oil
100ml/3½fl oz/generous ⅓ cup instant dashi (stock)
22.5ml/4½ tsp sake or dry white wine
15ml/1 tbsp mirin
22.5ml/4½ tsp soy sauce
22.5ml/4½ tsp sugar

1 Wash the hijiki seaweed thoroughly and soak it in cold water for 30 minutes. Drain well. Do not soak for any longer as it will lack flavour. During soaking, the hijiki will expand to about six times its dried volume.

2 Put the beancurd in a strainer and rinse it with hot water from a kettle to remove any excess oil. Then shred it into 3cm/1¼in long pieces. Shred the carrots and shiitake mushrooms into strips of about the same size.

3 Heat the oil in a large pan. Add the carrots, stir once, then add the shiitake mushrooms and stir-fry over a high heat for 1 minute. Add the hijiki, stir, then add the fried beancurd and stir-fry for 1 minute.

4 Pour in the stock, sake or wine, mirin and soy sauce. Stir in the sugar. Bring to the boil and reduce the heat, then simmer until all the soup has evaporated, stirring occasionally.

5 Serve the beancurd hot or cold, in four small bowls.

Cook's Tip

Hijiki is a dried seaweed with a high fibre content. If Japanese fried beancurd is not available, Chinese fried beancurd may be used instead.

Deep Fried Tofu and Asparagus in Stock

Agedashi is the name for dishes of deep fried (*age*) ingredients served in a stock (*dashi*) or thin sauce. Here, deep fried tofu and asparagus are served in a thin stock-based sauce and topped with tomato. A cup of sake goes very well with this *agedashi*.

INGREDIENTS

Serves 4

about ¹/₂ packet fresh Japanese tofu
   (10 x 5 x 3cm/4 x 2 x 1¹/₄in),
   200g/7oz weighed without water
4 asparagus spears, trimmed of tough
   stalk ends
1 beef tomato, skinned
cornflour, for coating
oil, for deep frying

For the sauce

200ml/7fl oz/scant 1 cup instant dashi
   (stock)
50ml/2fl oz/¹/₄ cup mirin
50ml/2fl oz/¹/₄ cup soy sauce

1 Wrap the tofu in a paper towel on a plate and cook in the microwave for 1 minute (600W) to remove excess water. Alternatively, wrap the tofu in a clean dish towel and press it between two plates for 30 minutes to remove excess moisture. Cut the tofu into eight cubes (about 2.5cm/1in each).

2 Cut the asparagus into 3–4cm/ 1¹/₄–1¹/₂in lengths. Halve the tomato and remove the seeds, then cut it into 5mm/¹/₄in cubes.

3 Slowly heat the oil for deep frying to 170°C/340°F. Coat the tofu with cornflour.

4 Deep fry the pieces in two batches over a medium heat until golden, allowing 7–10 minutes to ensure the tofu is cooked thoroughly. It starts to expand once it is cooked. Drain well. Keep the oil temperature at 170°C/340°F during cooking.

5 Meanwhile, place the ingredients for the sauce in a pan and bring to the boil, then simmer for 3 minutes. Deep fry the asparagus for 2 minutes and drain well.

6 Place the tofu on a large plate and arrange the asparagus on top. Pour on the hot sauce and sprinkle the tomato on top. Serve immediately.

Winter Tofu and Vegetables

This dish is brought bubbling hot to the table with a pot of dip to accompany the freshly cooked tofu and vegetables.

INGREDIENTS

Serves 4

1 sheet kombu seaweed (20 x 10cm/ 8 x 4in)
2 packets Japanese silken tofu (each 10 x 8 x 3cm/4 x 3¹/₄ x 1¹/₄in), about 600g/1lb 5oz
2 leeks
4 shiitake mushrooms, stems removed and cross cut in top
spring onions, chopped, to garnish

For the dip

200ml/7fl oz/scant 1 cup soy sauce
generous 15ml/1 tbsp mirin
100ml/3¹/₂fl oz/generous ¹/₃ cup bonito flakes

1 Half fill a large flameproof casserole or saucepan with cold water and soak the kombu seaweed in it for 30 minutes.

2 Cut the tofu into 4cm/1¹/₂in cubes. Slice the leek diagonally into 2cm/³/₄in thick slices.

3 To make the dip, bring the soy sauce and mirin to the boil, then add the bonito flakes. Remove from the heat and leave until all the flakes have sunk to the bottom of the pan, then strain the sauce and pour it into a small heatproof basin.

4 Stand the basin in the middle of the pan placing it on an upturned saucer, if necessary, so that it is well above the level of the water. This keeps the dip hot. Bring the water to the boil. Add the mushrooms and leeks, and cook over a moderate heat until softened – about 5 minutes. Then gently add the tofu. When the tofu starts floating, it is ready to eat. If the tofu won't all fit in the pan, it can be added during the meal.

5 Take the pan to the table and spoon the dip into four small bowls. Sprinkle the spring onions into the dip. Diners help themselves to tofu and vegetables from the pan and eat them with the dip. The kombu seaweed is used only to flavour the dish, it is not eaten.

Koya-tofu and Shiitake Stew

Koya-tofu takes its name from Mount Koya where tofu was frozen in the winter snows, then thawed. It is famous for being part of the diet of the Buddhist monks of the Koya temple. The process of freezing and thawing produces its characteristic texture.

INGREDIENTS

Serves 4
2 pieces dried Koya-tofu,
  15g/¹/₂oz each
8 dried shiitake mushrooms

For the soup
400ml/14fl oz/1²/₃ cups kombu and
  bonito stock or instant dashi
22.5ml/4¹/₂ tsp sake
30ml/2 tbsp mirin
2ml/¹/₃ tsp salt
15ml/1 tbsp usukuchi soy sauce

1 Cut a piece of foil just smaller than the saucepan.

2 Soak the dried Koya-tofu in tepid water for 30 minutes, then gently press out the water by hand. Soak the dried shiitake mushrooms in cold water for 20 minutes. Put a small saucer or plate on top to keep the mushrooms submerged. Drain the mushrooms and remove their stems.

3 Bring the stock to the boil and add the seasoning ingredients for the soup. Add the Koya-tofu, cover with a piece of folded foil on the surface of the liquid and simmer for 5–6 minutes.

4 Remove the foil. Add the drained shiitake mushrooms and simmer for a further 12–13 minutes. Leave the ingredients to cool in the soup.

5 To serve, cut the Koya-tofu into four pieces. Arrange these in a shallow bowl with the shiitake mushrooms. Serve warm or cold, but not chilled.

RICE AND NOODLE DISHES

Noodles, like tofu, originated in China and were subsequently adapted into Japanese cuisine. In Japan seasonality is very important in cooking and certain dishes are eaten at certain times of the year. For example, thin noodles are eaten in summer with just a little soy sauce and stock, whereas in winter thicker noodles are eaten, cooked in large casseroles.

Rice is a staple part of the Japanese diet and there are many different ways of cooking it. It can be boiled with stock and given a seasonal flavour by adding the fresh ingredients available at the time. It is usually eaten with every meal.

Individual Noodle Casseroles

Traditionally these individual casseroles are cooked in earthenware pots. *Nabe* means pot and *yaki* means to heat, providing the Japanese title of *Nabeyaki Udon* for this recipe.

INGREDIENTS

Serves 4

115g/4oz boneless chicken thigh
2.5ml/¹/₂ tsp salt
2.5ml/¹/₂ tsp sake or dry white wine
2.5ml/¹/₂ tsp soy sauce
1 leek
115g/4oz whole spinach, trimmed
300g/11oz dried udon noodles or 500g/1¹/₄lb fresh
4 shiitake mushrooms, stems removed
4 size 4 eggs
seven flavour spice (*shichimi*), to serve (optional)

For the soup

1.4 litres/2¹/₃ pints/6 cups kombu and bonito stock or instant dashi
22.5ml/4¹/₂ tsp soy sauce
7ml/1¹/₃ tsp salt
15ml/1 tbsp mirin

1 Cut the chicken into small chunks and sprinkle with the salt, sake or wine and soy sauce. Cut the leek diagonally into 4.5cm/1³/₄in slices.

2 Boil the spinach for 1–2 minutes, then drain and soak in cold water for 1 minute. Drain, squeeze lightly, then cut into 4cm/1¹/₂in lengths.

3 Boil dried udon according to the packet instruction, allowing 3 minutes less than the suggested cooking time. If using fresh udon, place them in boiling water, disentangle the noodles well and then drain them.

4 Bring the ingredients for the soup to the boil in a saucepan and add the chicken and leek. Skim the broth, then cook for 5 minutes. Divide the udon noodles between four individual flameproof casseroles. Pour the soup, chicken and leeks into the casseroles. Place over a moderate heat, then add the shiitake mushrooms.

5 Gently break an egg into each casserole. Cover and simmer for 2 minutes. Divide the spinach between the casseroles and simmer for 1 minute.

6 Serve immediately, standing the hot casseroles on plates or table mats. Sprinkle seven flavour spice over the casseroles if you like.

COOK'S TIP

Assorted tempura could be served in these casseroles instead of chicken and egg.

Five-flavour Noodles

The Japanese title for this dish is *Gomoku Yakisoba*, meaning five different ingredients; however, you can add as many different ingredients as you wish to make an exciting noodle stir-fry.

INGREDIENTS

Serves 4

300g/11oz dried Chinese thin egg noodles or 500g/1¼lb fresh yakisoba noodles
200g/7oz lean boneless pork, thinly sliced
22.5ml/4½ tsp oil
10g/¼oz fresh root ginger, grated
1 garlic clove, crushed
200g/7oz/1¾ cups green cabbage, roughly chopped
115g/4oz/½ cup bean sprouts
1 green pepper, seeded and cut into fine strips
1 red pepper, seeded and cut into fine strips
salt and white pepper
20ml/4 tsp ao-nori seaweed, to garnish (optional)

For the seasoning

60ml/4 tbsp Worcestershire sauce
15ml/1 tbsp soy sauce
15ml/1 tbsp oyster sauce
15ml/1 tbsp sugar
2.5ml/½ tsp salt

1 Boil the noodles according to the packet instruction and drain. Cut the pork into 3–4cm/1¼–1½in strips and season with salt and pepper.

2 Heat 7.5ml/1½ tsp oil in a large frying pan or a wok and stir-fry the pork until just cooked, then remove it from the pan.

4 Add the bean sprouts and stir until softened, then add the green and red peppers and stir-fry for 1 minute.

3 Wipe the pan with paper towel, and then heat the remaining oil in it. Add the ginger, garlic and cabbage and stir-fry for 1 minute.

5 Replace the pork in the pan and add the noodles. Stir in all the seasoning ingredients and season with white pepper. Stir-fry for 2–3 minutes.

6 Serve immediately, sprinkled with the ao-nori seaweed (if using).

Chicken and Egg with Rice

Oyako-don, the Japanese title for this dish means parent (*oya*), child (*ko*) and bowl (*don*); it is so called because it uses both chicken meat and egg. It is a classic dish which is eaten throughout the year.

INGREDIENTS

Serves 4
300g/11oz boneless chicken thighs
1 large mild onion, thinly sliced
200ml/7fl oz/scant 1 cup kombu and
    bonito stock or instant dashi
22.5ml/4¹⁄₂ tsp sugar
60ml/4 tbsp soy sauce
30ml/2 tbsp mirin
1kg/2¹⁄₄lb/7 cups freshly boiled rice
4–6 size 1 eggs, beaten
60ml/4 tbsp frozen peas, thawed
¹⁄₂ sheet yaki-nori seaweed, shredded,
    to garnish

1 Slice the chicken diagonally, then cut it into 3cm/1¹⁄₄ in lengths.

2 Place the onion, stock, sugar, soy sauce and mirin in a saucepan and bring to the boil. Add the chicken and cook over a moderate heat for about 5 minutes, or until the chicken is cooked. Skim any scum off the sauce.

3 Ladle a quarter of the mixture into a frying pan and bring to the boil.

4 Spoon a quarter of the rice into an individual serving bowl.

5 Pour a quarter of the egg over the mixture in the frying pan and sprinkle with a quarter of the peas. Cover and cook over a moderate heat until the egg is set to your taste.

6 Slide the cooked mixture on to the rice. Prepare the remaining three portions in the same way. Serve hot, sprinkled with the yaki-nori seaweed.

Steak Bowl

This appetizing dish looks very good at a dinner party and it is also very easy to prepare, leaving the cook time to relax.

INGREDIENTS

Serves 4
1 large mild onion
1 red pepper, seeded
30ml/2 tbsp oil
30ml/2 tbsp butter
400g/14oz sirloin steak, trimmed of
    excess fat
60ml/4 tbsp tomato ketchup
30ml/2 tbsp Worcestershire sauce
30ml/2 tbsp chopped parsley
1kg/2¹⁄₄lb/7 cups freshly boiled rice
salt and black pepper

For the garnish
bunch of watercress
a few red peppercorns (optional)

1 Cut the onion and red pepper into 7–8mm/¹⁄₃in slices.

2 Heat 15ml/1 tbsp oil in a frying pan and cook the onion until golden on both sides, adding salt and pepper, then set aside.

3 Heat 15ml/1 tbsp oil and 15ml/ 1 tbsp butter. Cook the steak over a high heat until browned on both sides, then cut it into bite-size pieces and set aside. For well-done steak, cook it over a moderate heat for 1–2 minutes each side.

4 For the sauce, mix the tomato ketchup, Worcestershire sauce and 30ml/2 tbsp water in the pan in which the steak was cooked. Stir over a moderate heat for 1 minute, mixing in the meat residue.

5 Mix the remaining butter and the chopped parsley into the hot rice. Divide between four serving bowls. Top the rice with the red pepper, onion and steak, and pour over the sauce. Garnish with watercress and red peppercorns (if using) and serve.

Sardine and Rice Bowl

INGREDIENTS

Serves 4

8 fresh sardines, scaled or frozen
    sardines, thawed
plain flour, for coating
15ml/1 tbsp oil, for cooking
2 green peppers, seeded and shredded
2 red peppers, seeded and shredded
1kg/2¼lb/7 cups freshly boiled rice
salt

For the marinade

15ml/1 tbsp soy sauce
7.5ml/1½ tsp sake or dry white wine
juice squeezed from 20g/¾oz grated
    fresh root ginger, about 5ml/1 tsp

For the sauce

30ml/2 tbsp sake or dry white wine
30ml/2 tbsp mirin
30ml/2 tbsp soy sauce
15ml/1 tbsp sugar

1 Cut the head off one sardine and lay it flat on a board. Slit the belly of the fish and take out the insides. Put both your thumbs in the middle of the fish and move one towards the head, the other towards the tail to open the fish. Snip the backbone near to the tail, then carefully lift it off the fish: the backbone should bring most small bones as you lift it off the fish. Discard all bones. Repeat the process with the remaining sardines.

2 Mix the marinade ingredients together in a large dish, turn the sardines in this, then leave to marinate for 20 minutes.

3 To make the sauce, bring the sake or wine and mirin to the boil, then add the soy sauce and sugar, and simmer for 3 minutes.

4 Remove the sardines from the marinade and sprinkle with flour.

5 Heat the oil in a frying pan. Cook the green and red peppers for 1 minute, until tender, season with salt, then set aside. Cook the sardines in the same pan, turning once, until golden on both sides.

6 Discard the oil and pour the sauce into the pan. Add the sardines and peppers, cook for 1 minute and then remove the pan from the heat.

7 Divide the hot rice between four serving bowls. Place two sardines on each portion. Divide the sauce and peppers between the dishes and serve immediately.

Chilled Noodles

This classic Japanese dish of cold noodles is known as *somen*. The noodles are surprisingly refreshing when eaten with the accompanying ingredients and a delicately flavoured dip. The noodles are served with ice to ensure that they remain chilled until they are eaten.

INGREDIENTS

Serves 4
oil, for cooking
2 size 4 eggs, beaten with a pinch of salt
1 sheet yaki-nori seaweed, finely shredded
½ bunch spring onions, thinly sliced
wasabi paste
400g/14oz dried somen noodles
ice cubes, for serving

For the dip
1 litre/1¾ pints/4 cups kombu and bonito stock or instant dashi
200ml/7fl oz/scant 1 cup soy sauce
15ml/1 tbsp mirin

1 Prepare the dip in advance so that it has time to cool and chill: bring the ingredients to the boil, then leave to cool and chill thoroughly.

2 Heat a little oil in a frying pan. Pour in half the egg, tilting the pan to coat the base evenly. Leave the egg to set, then turn it over and cook the second side briefly. Turn the omelette out on to a board. Cook the remaining egg in the same way.

3 Leave the omelettes to cool and then shred them finely. Place the shredded omelette, nori, spring onions and wasabi in four small bowls.

4 Boil the somen noodles according to the packet instructions and drain. Rinse the noodles in or under cold running water, stirring with chopsticks, then drain well.

5 Place the noodles on a large plate and add some ice cubes on top to keep them cool.

6 Pour the cold dip into four small bowls. Noodles and selected accompaniments are dipped into the chilled dip before they are eaten.

COOK'S TIP

Use scissors to finely shred the nori. Stir the noodles gently with chopsticks when rinsing them, as they are tender once cooked and easily damaged.

Japanese-style Hashed Beef

INGREDIENTS

Serves 4

300g/11oz beef topside, thinly sliced
15ml/1 tbsp oil
25g/1oz butter
450g/1lb onions, cut into 5mm/¼in
　thick slices
60ml/4 tbsp plain flour
200ml/7fl oz/scant 1 cup tomato
　ketchup
1 chicken stock cube, crumbled
22.5ml/4½ tsp Worcestershire sauce
15ml/1 tbsp red wine
30ml/2 tbsp frozen peas
1kg/2¼lb/7 cups freshly boiled rice
salt and pepper

1 Cut the beef into 3cm/1¼in
lengths and season them with salt
and pepper.

2 Heat the oil in a frying pan and
cook the beef until browned, then
transfer it to a flameproof casserole.

3 Heat the butter in the same frying
pan and cook the onions gently for
about 5 minutes. Sprinkle the flour
into the onions and cook, stirring, for
1–2 minutes. Stir in the ketchup, then
add the mixture to the beef.

4 Pour in 500ml/17fl oz/generous
2 cups water, add the stock cube
and stir well. Bring to the boil, skim
the broth, then reduce the heat.

5 Add the Worcestershire sauce and
red wine, then simmer for
30 minutes. Taste and adjust the
seasoning if necessary, then add the
peas and remove from the heat.

6 Divide the rice between four plates
and ladle the beef mixture on top.
Serve immediately.

Dry Curry

INGREDIENTS

Serves 4

1 small dried red chilli
1 small tomato, skinned
1 each green and red pepper, seeded
½ eating apple, peeled and cored
30ml/2 tbsp raisins
15ml/1 tbsp white wine
30ml/2 tbsp oil
15ml/1 tbsp butter
1 clove garlic, crushed
115g/4oz onion, finely chopped
300g/11oz minced beef
1kg/2¼lb/7 cups freshly boiled rice,
　to serve
cocktail gherkins, to garnish

For the seasoning

22.5ml/4½ tsp Japanese curry powder
10ml/2 tsp sugar
15ml/1 tbsp soy sauce
5ml/1 tsp salt

1 Soak the chilli in cold water for
5 minutes, then remove seeds and
slice finely. Dice the tomato, peppers
and the apple finely. Soak the raisins in
the white wine to soften them.

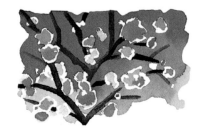

2 Heat the oil and butter in a
saucepan. Add the chilli, garlic and
onion, then cook until soft. Add the
minced beef, stir for 2–3 minutes to
break up, then mix in all the seasoning
ingredients. Stir for 4 minutes, add the
tomato, peppers, apple and raisins with
white wine and cook for 5–6 minutes.

3 Divide the rice between four plates
and spoon the dry curry on top.
Garnish with the gherkins and serve.

Mixed Rice

This recipe makes a very good party dish, and you can add a variety of ingredients to create your own special version.

INGREDIENTS

Serves 4
6 dried shiitake mushrooms
2 sheets fried tofu (*aburage*), each
13 x 6cm/5 x 2¹⁄₂in
6 mangetouts
1 carrot, cut into matchstick strips
115g/4oz chicken fillet, diced
30ml/2 tbsp sugar
37.5ml/7¹⁄₂ tsp soy sauce
1kg/2¹⁄₄lb/7 cups freshly boiled rice
salt

1 Soak the dried shiitake mushrooms in 800ml/27fl oz/3¹⁄₂ cups water for 30 minutes. Place a small plate or saucer on top of the mushrooms to keep them submerged.

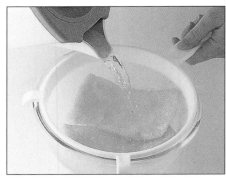

2 Put the fried tofu into a strainer and pour over hot water from a kettle to remove excess fat. Squeeze the tofu and cut it in half lengthways, then slice it into 5mm/¹⁄₄in wide strips.

3 Boil the mangetouts, drain and refresh in cold water and then drain well. Shred the mangetouts finely.

4 Drain the shiitake mushrooms, reserving the soaking water, remove their stems and finely slice the caps. Pour the soaking water into a saucepan. Add the tofu, carrot, chicken and shiitake mushrooms.

5 Bring to the boil, then skim the broth and simmer for 1–2 minutes. Add the sugar and cook for 1 minute, then add the soy sauce and salt. Simmer until most of the liquid has evaporated, leaving only a small amount of concentrated broth.

6 Mix in the hot rice, sprinkle the mangetouts over and serve the mixed rice at once.

Rice Balls

Picnics are very popular in Japan, where eating outdoors is considered to be great fun. Various cooked meals are taken on picnics, including rice balls, or *onigiri*. You can put anything you like in the rice, so you could invent your own onigiri.

INGREDIENTS

Serves 4 (8 rice balls)
15ml/1 tbsp salt
1kg/2¼lb/7 cups freshly boiled
 Japanese rice
4 umeboshi (plum pickles)
1 salmon steak, grilled
½ sheet yaki-nori seaweed
15ml/1 tbsp white or black sesame
 seeds

1 Put the salt in a bowl. Spoon an eighth of the rice into a small rice bowl. Make a hole in the middle and put in one umeboshi. Cover with rice.

2 Wet the palms of both hands with cold water, put a finger into the salt bowl and then rub the salt evenly on to your palms.

3 Empty the rice and umeboshi from the bowl on to one hand. Use both hands to shape the rice into a triangular shape, using firm but not heavy pressure. Make another three rice triangles in the same way.

4 Flake the salmon, discarding the skin and bones. Mix the fish into the remaining rice, then shape it into triangles as before.

5 Cut the yaki-nori into four even strips and wrap a strip around each of the umeboshi rice balls. Sprinkle sesame seeds on the salmon rice balls.

--- COOK'S TIP ---

Always use hot rice to make the balls, then allow them to cool completely and wrap each one in foil or clear film.

SUSHI

Once thought to be reserved for the rich and famous as the ultimate in fashionable eating, sushi is fast becoming popular for everyone. It is now more widely available through major supermarkets and delicatessens, so that many more people can enjoy this healthy food.

The fish for sushi must be absolutely fresh and the cooked rice cannot be kept in the fridge or it will go hard, so it is a dish that has to be eaten straightaway.

It takes many years of training to qualify as a sushi chef: the skills and techniques required are second to none.

Sushi is typically accompanied by wasabi (green freshwater horseradish) and soy sauce.

Shaped Sushi

INGREDIENTS

Serves 4

480g/1lb 1oz/2¹/₅ cups Japanese rice, washed and drained for 1 hour
30ml/2 tbsp sake or dry white wine
wasabi paste
salt
soy sauce and gari, to serve

For the sushi vinegar

60ml/4 tbsp rice vinegar
15ml/1 tbsp sugar

For the seafood garnish

1 squid body sack, skinned (about 200g/7oz total weight)
1 leg boiled octopus
200g/7oz block tuna for sashimi
200g/7oz block salmon for sashimi
4 raw large prawns, heads removed

For the marinade

15ml/1 tbsp rice vinegar
5ml/1 tsp sugar

For the Rolled Omelette

3 eggs
15ml/1 tbsp each of sake or dry white wine, sugar and water
1cm/¹/₂in strip yakinori seaweed

1 Cook the rice, replacing 30ml/2 tbsp of the measured cooking water with the sake or wine. Meanwhile, heat the ingredients for the sushi vinegar, adding 5ml/1 tsp salt, stir well and cool. Add this to the hot cooked rice, stir well with a spatula, at the same time fanning the rice constantly – this gives the rice an attractive glaze. Cover with a damp cloth and leave to cool. Do not put in the refrigerator, as this will make the rice go hard.

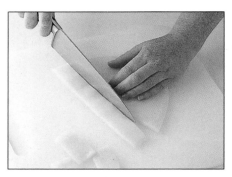

2 Cut the squid into strips measuring 2–3cm/³/₄–1¹/₄in wide and 5cm/2in long. Slice the octopus leg into strips of the same size. Cut the tuna and salmon into pieces of similar size, but about 3mm/¹/₈in thick.

3 Thread the prawns on to bamboo skewers from tail to head to make sure they lay flat when cooked. Boil for just 1 minute, then remove the skewers and shells, leaving the tails intact. Slit each prawn along the belly, taking care not to cut right through, and remove the dark vein, then open it up like a book. Mix the marinade ingredients in a dish, adding a pinch of salt, add the prawns and leave for 10 minutes.

4 Make a Rolled Omelette with the ingredients listed, adding 2ml/¹/₃ tsp salt. Cool, then slice into 5mm/¹/₄in thick pieces.

5 Wet your hands, then shape about 15–20g/¹/₂–³/₄oz rice into a rectangle measuring 1cm/¹/₂in high, 2cm/³/₄in wide and 5cm/2in long. Repeat with the remaining rice.

6 Use your finger to spread a little wasabi on the middle of the rice oblongs and lay the seafood on top. Do not add wasabi for egg sushi but tie together with the seaweed. Serve with soy sauce, and gari to cleanse the palate after each mouthful.

Simple Rolled Sushi

To perfect the art of rolling sushi in seaweed takes practice and there is no better way than by starting with this simple form of rolled sushi, known as *Hosomaki*, which is usually a slim roll with only one filling. It is very good for picnics and canapés as the pieces are so easy to eat and, of course, this type of sushi is always served cold. You will need a bamboo mat (*makisu*) for the rolling process.

INGREDIENTS

Makes 12 rolls or 72 slices
6 sheets yaki-nori seaweed

For the filling
200g/7oz block tuna for sashimi
200g/7oz block salmon for sashimi
1/2 cucumber, quartered lengthways and
    seeds removed
wasabi paste

For the rice
400g/14oz/2 cups Japanese rice,
    cooked as for Shaped Sushi, using
    Mixed Vinegar (below)

For the Mixed Vinegar
52.5ml/10 1/2 tsp rice vinegar
15ml/1 tbsp sugar
3ml/2/3 tsp salt
gari (ginger pickles), to garnish
soy sauce, to serve

1 Cut the nori in half lengthways. Cut the tuna and salmon into four, 1cm/1/2in square, long sticks. The sticks should be the same length as the long side of the nori. Use two sticks per nori if necessary.

2 Place a sheet of nori, shiny side downwards, on a bamboo mat on a chopping board.

3 Divide the rice in half in its bowl, then mark each half into six, making 12 portions in all. Spread one portion of the rice over the nori with your fingers, leaving a 1cm/1/2in space uncovered at the top and bottom of the nori.

4 Spread a little wasabi in a horizontal line along the middle of the rice and lay a stick of tuna on this.

5 Holding the mat and the edge of the nori nearest to you, roll up the nori and rice into a tube with the tuna in the middle. Use the mat as a guide – do not roll it into the food. Roll the rice tightly so that it sticks together and encloses the filling firmly.

6 Carefully roll the sushi off the mat. Make 11 other rolls in the same way, four for each filling ingredient. Do not use wasabi with the cucumber. Use a wet knife to cut each roll into six slices and stand them on a platter. Wipe and re-rinse the knife occasionally between cuts. Garnish with gari (ginger pickles) and serve soy sauce with the sushi.

Mixed Rice Sushi

INGREDIENTS

Serves 4

2 sheets fried tofu (*aburage*)
4 dried shiitake mushrooms, soaked
200ml/7fl oz/scant 1 cup plus 15ml/
  1 tbsp instant dashi (stock)
50ml/10 tsp sugar
15ml/1 tbsp usukuchi soy sauce
1 carrot, cut into matchstick strips
10ml/2 tsp soy sauce
1 quantity rice as for Shaped Sushi
50g/2oz fresh or canned lotus root,
  peeled, and thinly sliced
50ml/2floz/¼ cup rice vinegar
30ml/2 tbsp sake or dry white wine
12 raw large prawns, thawed if frozen,
  heads removed
oil, for cooking
30ml/2 tbsp ground white sesame seeds
20 mangetouts, boiled and thinly sliced
salt

For the sushi vinegar

60ml/4 tbsp rice vinegar
20ml/4 tsp sugar
5ml/1 tsp salt

For the omelette

2 eggs, beaten
15ml/1 tbsp sake or dry white wine
10ml/2 tsp sugar

1 Rinse the tofu in hot water. Drain and slice finely. Drain the shiitake mushrooms, remove the stems and slice.

2 Pour the main quantity of stock into a saucepan. Add 15ml/1 tbsp sugar, the usukuchi soy sauce and carrot, and simmer for 5 minutes. Lift out the carrots. Stir in 15ml/1 tbsp sugar and the soy sauce, then add the tofu and shiitake mushrooms, and simmer until the liquid has evaporated. Leave to cool. Cook the rice, then add the sushi vinegar as for Shaped Sushi.

3 If using fresh lotus root, soak in plenty of water with 5ml/1 tsp rice vinegar added for 5 minutes to remove bitter flavours. Bring 30ml/2 tbsp rice vinegar, the sake or wine, 15ml/1 tbsp sugar and a pinch of salt to the boil. Add the drained lotus root and simmer for 5 minutes or until there is just a little liquid left. Leave to cool.

4 Boil the prawns for 1 minute, then drain and shell them, leaving their tails intact. Mix the remaining 15ml/1 tbsp each of rice vinegar and stock, 5ml/1 tsp sugar and a pinch of salt. Add the prawns and set aside.

5 Make four thin omelettes: mix the eggs, sake or wine, sugar and a pinch of salt. Heat a little oil in a pan and pour in a quarter of the mixture, tilting the pan to coat it evenly. Turn the omelette when set and cook the second side, then transfer it to a plate. Pile up the omelettes, roll up and slice them thinly into fine shreds.

6 Mix the carrot, tofu, mushrooms and ground sesame seeds into the rice using a cutting action, rather than stirring, to avoid breaking up the grains. Serve in one large dish or four plates. Top with the drained prawns, lotus root, omelette shreds and mangetouts. Serve immediately.

Tuna Rice Bowl

One of the most popular dishes in Japan, *Tekka-don* consists of rice with fresh tuna laid on top.

INGREDIENTS

Serves 4

300g/11oz block tuna for sashimi
1 sheet yaki-nori seaweed
1 quantity rice as for Shaped Sushi,
  cooked and cooled to room
  temperature

For the accompaniments

wasabi paste and soy sauce

1 Slice the tuna in the same way as for Sliced Raw Salmon but making the slices thinner.

2 Using scissors, cut the nori seaweed into 4–5cm/1½–2in strips.

3 The rice must be at room temperature, so as not to cook the tuna: divide it between four bowls. Arrange the tuna on top of the rice and sprinkle the seaweed over. Serve immediately, with wasabi and soy sauce.

Rolled Sushi with Mixed Filling

INGREDIENTS

Makes 32 pieces

For the filling

4 large dried shiitake mushrooms
1 small carrot, quartered lengthways
1 chikuwa fish cake or 4 crab sticks, cut
    into strips as for the carrot
½ cucumber, quartered lengthways,
    seeds removed
4 sheets yaki-nori seaweed, for rolling
soy sauce and gari (ginger pickles),
    to serve

For the seasoning

37.5ml/7½ tsp soy sauce
15ml/1 tbsp each of mirin, sake or dry
    white wine and sugar

For the Rolled Omelette

2 size 1 eggs
10ml/2 tsp sugar
pinch of salt

For the rice

320g/11½oz/1½ cups Japanese rice,
    cooked as for Shaped Sushi, using
    Mixed Vinegar (below)

For the Mixed Vinegar

40ml/8 tsp rice vinegar
22.5ml/4½ tsp sugar
3ml/⅔ tsp salt

1 Soak the shiitake in 200ml/
7fl oz/scant 1 cup water for
30 minutes; drain, reserving the stock,
and remove their stems. Pour the stock
into a saucepan, add the seasoning
ingredients and simmer the carrots,
mushrooms and chikuwa or crab sticks
for 4–5 minutes. Remove the carrots
and chikuwa or crab sticks. Simmer the
shiitake until all the liquid has
evaporated, then thinly slice them.
Make the Rolled Omelette.

2 Place a bamboo mat (*makisu*) on a
chopping board. Lay a sheet of
nori, shiny side down, lengthways.

3 Spread a quarter of the prepared,
dressed rice over the nori using
your fingers, leaving a 1cm/½in space
at the top and bottom.

4 Place a quarter of each of the filling
ingredients across the middle of the
layer of rice.

5 Carefully hold the nearest edge of
the nori and the mat, then roll up
the nori using the mat as a guide to
make a neat tube of rice with the filling
ingredients in the middle. Roll the rice
tightly to ensure that the grains stick
together and to keep the filling in
place. Roll the sushi off the mat and
make three more rolls in the same way.

6 Using a wet knife, cut each roll
into eight pieces and stand them
upright on a platter. Serve soy sauce
and gari with the sushi.

COOK'S TIP

When cutting sushi, use a large cook's
knife and rinse it with cold water. To
prevent the rice from sticking to the knife,
wipe the blade and rinse it under cold
water between cuts - or at least after every
few cuts.

Tofu-wrapped Sushi

This is another popular picnic dish, particularly with children who like its slightly sweet flavour. The tofu should be prepared while the rice is cooking (or beforehand) as the rice has to be warm so that it can be packed into the tofu. Wasabi is not used for this *Inari-sushi*.

INGREDIENTS

Makes 12
6 sheets fried tofu (*aburage*)
200ml/7fl oz/scant 1 cup kombu and
  bonito stock or instant dashi
45ml/3 tbsp sugar
37.5ml/7$^1/_2$ tsp soy sauce
30ml/2 tbsp sake or dry white wine
30ml/2 tbsp mirin
dash of rice vinegar
gari (ginger pickles), to garnish

For the rice
240g/8$^1/_2$oz/1$^1/_8$ cups Japanese rice
15ml/1 tbsp sake

For the sushi vinegar
30ml/2 tbsp rice vinegar
15ml/1 tbsp sugar
2.5ml/$^1/_2$ tsp salt

1 Lay a sheet of fried tofu on a board. Using a chopstick as a rolling pin, roll the tofu, this will ensure that it opens easily when boiled. Bring a large saucepan of water to the boil and blanch the tofu to remove excess fat, then drain and squeeze it. Cut the sheets of tofu in half widthways, then carefully open out with a knife to make 12 small sacks or pockets.

2 Bring the stock, sugar, soy sauce, sake or wine, mirin and rice vinegar to the boil. Add the tofu, cover with folded foil and simmer until the liquid has virtually evaporated, pressing the foil down occasionally to squeeze the soup from the tofu and prevent the packets from filling. Drain and cool. Heat the ingredients for the sushi vinegar and leave to cool.

3 Cook the rice, replacing 15ml/ 1 tbsp of the measured cooking water with the sake. Add the sushi vinegar to the rice and stir well with a spatula. Divide the warm rice between the tofu and fold the tofu to enclose the rice in neat parcels. Arrange on plates with the folded sides underneath and serve garnished with gari.

SOUPS

There are two basic types of soup in Japan: one comes from the eastern part and uses stock made from wakame seaweed and bonito flakes; the other comes from the west and uses stock made from dried baby sardines. Soup always accompanies a special dish and the two are eaten together.

There are no set courses in Japan: all dishes are eaten together. Soup is also eaten for breakfast, when it is typically served with seaweed and a soft-boiled egg.

Pork and Vegetable Soup

INGREDIENTS

Serves 4

50g/2oz gobo (optional)
5ml/1 tsp rice vinegar
1/2 black konnyaku, 125g/4 1/4oz
10ml/2 tsp oil
200g/7oz belly pork, cut into thin
    3–4cm/1 1/4–1 1/2in long strips
115g/4oz mooli (daikon radish), peeled
    and thinly sliced
50g/2oz carrot, thinly sliced
1 medium potato, thinly sliced
4 shiitake mushrooms, stems removed
    and thinly sliced
800ml/27fl oz/3 1/2 cups kombu and
    bonito stock or instant dashi
15ml/1 tbsp sake or dry white wine
45ml/3 tbsp red or white miso paste

For the garnish
2 spring onions, thinly sliced
seven spice flavour (*shichimi*)

1 Scrub the skin off the gobo, if using, with a vegetable brush. Slice the vegetable into fine shavings. Soak the prepared gobo for 5 minutes in plenty of water with the vinegar added to remove any bitter taste, then drain.

2 Put the piece of konnyaku in a small pan and add enough water just to cover it. Bring to the boil over a moderate heat, then drain and allow to cool. This removes any bitter taste.

3 Using your hands, tear the konnyaku into 2cm/3/4in lumps. Do not use a knife as a smooth cut surface will not absorb any flavour.

4 Heat the oil in a deep saucepan and quickly stir-fry the pork. Add all the gobo, mooli, carrot, potato, shiitake mushrooms and konnyaku, then stir-fry for one minute. Pour in the stock and sake or wine.

5 Bring the soup to the boil, then skim it and simmer for 10 minutes, until the vegetables have softened.

6 Ladle a little of the soup into a small bowl and dissolve the miso paste in it. Pour the mixture back into the saucepan and bring to the boil once more. Do not continue to boil or the flavour will be lost. Remove from the heat, then pour into serving bowls. Sprinkle with the spring onions and seven spice flavour, and serve immediately.

Mixed Vegetable Soup

The main ingredient for this soup is crushed tofu, which is both nutritious and satisfying.

INGREDIENTS

Serves 4

150g/5oz fresh tofu, weighed without water
2 dried shiitake mushrooms
50g/2oz gobo
5ml/1 tsp rice vinegar
1/2 black or white konnyaku, 125g/4¼oz
30ml/2 tbsp sesame oil
115g/4oz mooli (daikon radish), thinly sliced
50g/2oz carrot, thinly sliced
700ml/24fl oz/scant 3 cups kombu and bonito stock or instant dashi
pinch of salt
30ml/2 tbsp sake or dry white wine
7.5ml/1½ tsp mirin
45ml/3 tbsp white or red miso paste
dash of soy sauce
6 mangetouts, trimmed, boiled and thinly sliced, to garnish

1 Crush the tofu by hand until it resembles a lumpy scrambled egg texture – do not crush it too finely.

2 Wrap the tofu in a dish towel and put it in a strainer, then pour over plenty of boiling water. Leave the tofu to drain thoroughly for 10 minutes.

3 Soak the dried shiitake mushrooms in tepid water for 20 minutes, then drain them. Remove their stems, and cut the caps into 4–6 pieces. Reserve the soaking water for stock.

4 Use a vegetable brush to scrub the skin off the gobo and slice it into thin shavings. Soak the shavings for 5 minutes in plenty of cold water with the vinegar added to remove any bitter taste. Drain well.

5 Put the konnyaku in a small saucepan and pour over just enough water to cover it. Bring to the boil over a moderate heat, then drain and allow to cool. Using your hands, tear the konnyaku into 2cm/³⁄₄in lumps. Do not use a knife as smooth cuts will prevent it from absorbing flavour.

6 Heat the sesame oil in a deep saucepan. Add all the shiitake mushrooms, gobo, mooli, carrot and konnyaku. Stir-fry for 1 minute, then add the tofu and stir well.

7 Pour in the stock and add the salt, sake or wine and mirin. Bring to the boil. Skim the broth and simmer it for 5 minutes.

8 In a small bowl, dissolve the miso paste in a little of the soup, then return it to the pan. Simmer the soup gently for 10 minutes, until the vegetables are soft. Add the soy sauce, then remove from the heat. Serve immediately in four bowls, garnished with the mangetouts.

Miso Soup

This soup is one of the most commonly eaten dishes in Japan, and it is usually served with every meal which includes rice. Every family has its unique recipe for this soup, with individual ingredient combinations.

INGREDIENTS

Serves 4

$^1/_2$ packet silken tofu (10 x 5 x 3cm/ 4 x 2 x 1$^1/_4$in), about 150g/5oz weighed without water
800ml/27fl oz/3$^1/_2$ cups kombu and bonito stock or instant dashi
10g/$^1/_4$oz dried wakame seaweed
60ml/4 tbsp white or red miso paste
2 spring onions, chopped, to garnish

1 Cut the tofu into 1cm/$^1/_2$in cubes. Bring the stock to the boil and reduce the heat.

2 Add the wakame seaweed and simmer for 1–2 minutes. Pour some soup into a bowl and add the miso paste, stirring so that it dissolves. Pour the mixture back into the pan.

3 Add the tofu and heat through for 1 minute, then serve immediately. Garnish with chopped spring onions.

—————— COOK'S TIP ——————

Reduce the heat when the stock boils as it loses flavour if boiled for too long. Similarly, cook the soup long enough to heat the ingredients.

Shiitake Mushroom and Egg Soup

Osumashi means clear soup and this Shiitake and Egg Osumashi goes particularly well with any sushi, as its delicate flavour complements, rather than overpowers, especially the flavour of the fish.

INGREDIENTS

Serves 4

600ml/1 pint/2$^1/_2$ cups kombu and bonito stock or instant dashi
4 shiitake mushrooms, stems removed and thinly sliced
5 ml/1 tsp salt
10ml/2 tsp usukuchi soy sauce
5ml/1 tsp sake or dry white wine
2 size 4 eggs
$^1/_2$ punnet cress, to garnish

1 Bring the stock to the boil, add the shiitake mushrooms and simmer for 1–2 minutes but do not over cook.

2 Add the salt, usukuchi soy sauce and sake or wine. Then break the eggs into a bowl and stir well with chopsticks.

3 Pour the egg into the soup in a thin steady stream, in a circular motion – rather like drawing a spiral shape in the soup. To keep the soup clear, the heat must be high enough to set the egg as soon as it is added

4 Simmer for a few seconds until the eggs are cooked. Use a pair of chopsticks to break up the egg in order to serve it equally between four bowls. Remove from the heat. Sprinkle with cress and serve immediately.

Prawn and Egg-knot Soup

INGREDIENTS

Serves 4

800ml/27fl oz/3½ cups kombu and bonito stock or instant dashi
5ml/1 tsp usukuchi soy sauce
salt
1 spring onion, thinly sliced, to garnish

For the prawn shinjo balls

200g/7oz raw large prawns, shelled, thawed if frozen
65g/2½oz cod fillet, skinned
5ml/1 tsp egg white
5ml/1 tsp plus a dash of sake or dry white wine
22.5ml/4½ tsp cornflour or potato starch (*katakuri-ko*)
2–3 drops soy sauce

For the omelette

1 egg, beaten
dash of mirin
oil, for cooking

1 Remove the black vein running down the back of the prawns. Process the prawns, cod, egg white, 5ml/1 tsp sake or wine, cornflour or potato starch, soy sauce and a pinch of salt in a food processor or blender to make a sticky paste. Alternatively, finely chop the prawns and cod, crush them with the knife's blade and then pound them well in a mortar with a pestle, adding the remaining ingredients.

2 Shape the mixture into four balls and steam them for 10 minutes over a high heat. Soak the spring onion in cold water for 5 minutes, then drain.

3 Mix the egg with a pinch of salt and the mirin. Heat a little oil in a frying pan and pour in the egg, tilting the pan to coat it evenly. When the egg has set, turn the omelette over and cook for 30 seconds. Leave to cool.

4 Cut the omelette into long strips, 2cm/¾in wide. Knot each strip once, place in a strainer and rinse with hot water to remove excess oil. Bring the stock to the boil and add the usukuchi soy sauce, a pinch of salt and a dash of sake or wine. Divide the prawn balls and the egg knots among four bowls. Pour in the soup, sprinkle with the spring onion and serve.

Fish Ball Soup

Tsumire means, quite literally, sardine balls and these are added to this delicious *Tsumire-jiru* soup to impart their robust fish flavour. This is a warming and nutritious dish for winter.

INGREDIENTS

Serves 4

20g/³⁄₄oz fresh root ginger
800g/1³⁄₄lb fresh sardines, gutted and
   heads removed
30ml/2 tbsp white miso paste
15ml/1 tbsp sake or dry white wine
7.5ml/¹⁄₂ tbsp sugar
1 egg
30ml/2 tbsp cornflour
150g/5oz shimeji mushrooms or 6
   shiitake mushrooms
1 leek or large spring onion

For the soup

100ml/3¹⁄₂fl oz/generous ¹⁄₃ cup sake
   or dry white wine
1.2 litres/2 pints/5 cups instant dashi
   (stock)
60ml/4 tbsp white miso paste

1 First make the fish balls. Grate the ginger and squeeze it well to yield 5ml/1 tsp ginger juice.

2 Rinse the sardines under cold running water, then cut in half along the backbone. Remove all the bones. To skin a boned sardine, lay it skin side down on a board, then run a sharp knife slowly along the skin from tail to head.

3 Coarsely chop the sardines and process with the ginger juice, miso, sake or wine, sugar and egg to a thick paste in a food processor or blender. Transfer to a bowl and mix in the cornflour well.

4 Trim the shimeji mushrooms and separate each stem or remove the stems from the shiitake mushrooms and shred them. Cut the leek or spring onion into 4cm/1¹⁄₂in long strips.

5 Bring the ingredients for the soup to the boil. Use two wet spoons to shape small portions of the sardine mixture into bite-sized balls and drop them into the soup. Add the mushrooms and leeks or spring onions.

6 Simmer until the sardine balls float to the surface. Serve immediately, in four deep bowls.

SWEETS

Japan has always been a relatively poor country and sweets were once seen as a luxury, only to be served on special occasions, such as festivals and tea ceremonies. Nowadays, sweets are more commonly eaten but are made without any of the dairy ingredients used in western desserts. Instead, lots of bean products are used, such as aduki bean paste.

Rice cakes are a popular dessert. For these, the rice is steamed and then pounded until sticky before being wrapped round a centre of aduki bean paste.

Green Tea Cake

Baking cakes for desserts takes on a new twist when using Japanese ingredients. For example, glacé aduki beans are used in the same way as marrons glacés and the cake remains moist and light.

INGREDIENTS

Makes a 18 x 7.5 x 10cm/7 x 3 x 4in loaf tin

115g/4oz/1 cup plain flour
15g/¹/₂oz green tea powder
2.5ml/¹/₂ tsp baking powder
3 size 3 eggs
75g/3oz/¹/₃ cup granulated sugar
75g/3oz/¹/₃ cup ama-natto (glacé Japanese aduki beans)
65g/2¹/₂oz/5 tbsp lightly salted butter, melted
whipped cream, to serve (optional)

1 Preheat the oven to 180°C/350°F/Gas 4. Line and grease a loaf tin. Sift the flour, green tea powder and baking powder together and set aside.

2 In a large heatproof bowl, whisk the eggs and sugar over a saucepan of hot water until pale and thick.

3 Sprinkle the sifted flour over the mixture. Before the flour sinks into the mixture, add the Japanese glacé aduki beans, then fold in the ingredients gently using a spatula. Fold the mixture over from the bottom once or twice. Do not mix too hard. Fold in the melted butter.

4 Pour the mixture into the tin and smooth the top. Bake in the lower part of the oven for 35–40 minutes or until a warm metal skewer inserted into the centre of the cake comes out free of sticky mixture. Turn out the cake on to a wire rack and remove the lining paper while it is hot. Leave to cool. Slice and serve with whipped cream, if you like.

Rice Cakes with Strawberries

Whereas traditionally an ingredient such as aduki bean paste would have been the sole accompaniment for these rice cakes, in this fairly modern dessert, fresh fruit is also served.

INGREDIENTS

Makes 5

100g/3¾oz/scant ½ cup shiratama-ko powder
15ml/1 tbsp granulated sugar
cornflour, for coating
10 strawberries
115g/4oz/scant ½ cup canned *neri-an* (Japanese soft aduki bean paste), cut into 5 pieces

1 In a microwaveproof bowl, mix the shiratama-ko powder and sugar. Gradually add 200ml/7fl oz/scant 1 cup water, then knead well to make a thick paste.

2 Cover and cook in a microwave for 1½–2 minutes (600 or 500W). Alternatively, steam the mixture in a bowl over a saucepan of simmering water for 10–15 minutes.

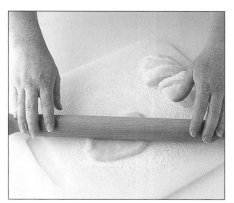

3 Lightly dust a chopping board with cornflour. Turn out the mixture on to it and divide it into five pieces. Roll out a portion of mixture into a small oval shape.

4 Put a strawberry and a piece of *neri-an* in the middle. Fold the rice cake in half and serve decorated with a strawberry. Make a further four rice cakes. Eat the rice cakes on the day they are prepared – if left for any longer they will harden.

Sweet Aduki Bean Soup with Rice Cakes

This is another well-known classic Japanese dessert – *Zenzai* is a really sweet aduki bean soup and is served with rice cakes. Ready-to-eat rice cakes (*mochi*) can be found in most Japanese supermarkets.

INGREDIENTS

Serves 4

165g/5¹/₂oz/scant 1 cup dried aduki beans
185–200g/6¹/₂–7oz/about 1 cup granulated sugar
pinch of salt
4 ready-to-eat rice cakes (*mochi*)

1 Wash the aduki beans in cold running water, then drain them and place in a large saucepan. Add 1 litre/1³/₄ pints/4 cups water and bring to the boil. Drain the beans and replace them in the pan. Add 1.2 litres/ 2 pints/5 cups water and bring to the boil, then add a further 100ml/ 3¹/₂fl oz/generous ¹/₃ cup water and bring it to the boil again. Simmer for 30 minutes until the beans are softened. Skim the broth constantly to ensure that it does not have a bitter taste.

2 When the beans are soft enough to be mashed between your fingers, add half the sugar and simmer for a further 20 minutes. Then add the remaining sugar and the salt, and stir until dissolved.

3 Grill both sides of the rice cakes until softened. Add the rice cakes to the soup and bring to the boil. Serve immediately in four deep bowls. Japanese green tea goes well with this dessert.

Caramelized Sweet Potatoes

Caramelized sweet potatoes are delicious served hot or cold.

INGREDIENTS

Serves 4

500g/1¹/₄lb sweet potato
oil, for deep frying
115g/4oz/generous ¹/₂ cup granulated sugar
15ml/1 tbsp golden syrup or Japanese syrup (*mizu-ame*)
black sesame seeds, to decorate

1 Thickly peel the potatoes and cut them into bite-size narrow pieces, then soak them in cold water for 5 minutes.

2 Slowly heat the oil for deep frying to 170°C/340°F. Wipe the potatoes well on paper towels and deep fry them slowly until golden. Drain the potatoes well.

3 In a large frying pan, heat the sugar and 45ml/3 tbsp water until caramelized. Add the syrup and mix.

4 Add the potatoes to the caramel and turn them to coat them thoroughly. Remove from the heat and sprinkle with the sesame seeds.

Green and Yellow Layered Cakes

This colourful two-tone dessert is made by squeezing contrasting mixtures in a small pouch of muslin or thin cotton. The Japanese title is derived from the preparation technique: *chakin-shibori*, in which *chakin* means a pouch shape and *shibori* means a moulding action.

INGREDIENTS

Makes 6

For the yolk mixture (kimi–an)
6 size 2 eggs
50g/2oz/¼ cup granulated sugar

For the pea mixture (endo–an)
200g/7oz/1¾ cups fresh peas, shelled
40g/1½oz/8 tsp sugar

1 To make the yolk mixture, hard boil the eggs. Remove the yolks and sieve them into a bowl. Press the yolk with a spatula, add the sugar and mix well.

2 To make the pea mixture, boil the peas for about 15 minutes, or until softened. Drain and place in a mortar, then crush the peas with a pestle and transfer them to a saucepan.

3 Add the sugar and cook, stirring continuously, until the paste is thick. Keep the mixture simmering but ensure that it does not scorch on the bottom of the pan.

4 Spread out the paste in a large dish to cool it down quickly. To maintain its green colour, it is important to cool the paste as quickly as possible.

5 Divide each of the mixtures into six portions. Wet a piece of muslin or thin cotton and wring it out well.

6 Place a lump of pea mixture on the cloth and put a lump of the yolk mixture on top. Wrap the mixture up and squeeze the top of the cloth to mark an attractive spiral pattern on the top of the cakes. Squeezing the cloth also joins the two stuffings together. Make another five cakes in the same way. Serve cold.

Sweet Potato, Apple and Bean Paste Cakes

A mixture of mashed sweet potato and a hint of apple is shaped into cubes, covered in batter and then seared in a hot pan to seal in the natural moisture. Aduki bean paste is also made into cakes by the same method.

INGREDIENTS

Serves 3 (makes 6)
about 250g/9oz canned neri-an (Japanese soft aduki bean paste), divided into 3 pieces

For the batter
90ml/6 tbsp plain flour
pinch of sugar
75ml/5 tbsp water

For the sweet potato and apple stuffing
150g/5oz sweet potato, peeled
¼ red eating apple, cored and peeled
200ml/7fl oz/scant 1 cup water
50g/2oz/¼ cup sugar
¼ lemon

3 Coarsely chop the apple and place in a saucepan. Add the water and sweet potato. Sprinkle in 7.5ml/1½ tsp sugar and cook over a moderate heat until the apple and potato are softened.

6 Heat a non-stick frying pan. Coat a cube of mixture in batter, then, taking great care not to burn your fingers, sear each side of the cube on the hot pan until the batter has set and cooked.

7 Repeat this procedure with the remaining mixture and with the *neri-an*, shaped into similar-sized cubes. Arrange one of each type of cake on a small plate and serve hot or cold.

1 Put all the ingredients for the batter in a bowl and mix well until smooth. Pour the batter into a large, shallow dish.

2 Dice the sweet potato and soak it in plenty of cold water for 5 minutes to remove any bitterness, then drain well.

4 Add the lemon juice and remove the pan from the heat. Then drain the sweet potato and apple and crush them to a coarse paste with the remaining sugar in a bowl.

5 Using your hands, shape the mixture into three cubes.

PARTY MEALS

Home entertaining is a very important part of Japanese social life. A great many dishes are cooked at the table in front of the guests who actively participate in the cooking of their meal. It is a unique and fun experience to have a bubbling hot pot or sizzling grill cooking your food in front of your eyes. There is also a form of sushi served at the table, where guests are supplied with their own ingredients, so that they can make their own individual combinations. This, too, is great fun, as every guest becomes involved.

Beef and Vegetables on a Hot Plate

This is *Yakiniku*, a dish of beef cooked at the table – you will need a portable griddle or grill pan and you can cook a variety of different ingredients, such as chicken or fish.

INGREDIENTS

Serves 4

1 red oak lettuce
1 mooli (daikon radish), finely grated
oil, for cooking
400g/14oz beef topside, very thinly sliced
1 red pepper, seeded and sliced
1 green pepper, seeded and sliced
1 large mild onion, sliced into rings
4 shiitake mushrooms, stems removed
1 carrot, thinly sliced
8 raw tiger prawns, heads removed, shelled, with tails left on
soy sauce, for serving

For the ponzu dip
100ml/3¹/₂fl oz/generous ¹/₃ cup each of lemon juice, soy sauce and instant dashi (stock)

1 Prepare the ponzu dip by mixing the ingredients. Divide the dip between small individual serving bowls. Separate the lettuce leaves and arrange them on plates.

2 Gently squeeze the grated mooli to remove any excess water. Put 15–30ml/1–2 tbsp mooli into small individual bowls and pour on a little soy sauce.

3 Heat the grill or hot plate on a thick mat to protect the table. Add a little oil and quickly grill the beef until cooked on both sides. Grill the peppers, onion, mushrooms, carrot and prawns at the same time.

4 To eat the food, wrap individual portions in lettuce leaves and dip them into the ponzu or mooli dip. Alternatively, the food may be dipped without being wrapped in the lettuce leaves if preferred.

Sukiyaki

You will need a chafing dish and burner or portable gas or electric cooker for this dish as it is cooked at the table. A sukiyaki meal is great fun because your guests can watch their dinner cooking in front of them, then they can help themselves to the delicious delicacies.

INGREDIENTS

Serves 4

1kg/2¼lb beef topside, very thinly
   sliced
lard, for cooking
4 leeks or Japanese spring onions (*negi*),
   sliced diagonally into pieces
   1cm/½in thick
bunch of *shungiku* leaves, stems
   removed and coarsely chopped
   (optional)
bunch of enoki mushrooms, brown
   roots cut off (optional)
8 shiitake mushrooms, stems removed
300g/11oz shirataki noodles, boiled for
   2 minutes, drained and halved
2 pieces yaki tofu, 10 x 7cm/4 x 2¾in,
   cut into 3cm/1¼in cubes
4–8 fresh eggs, to serve

For the sukiyaki stock

100ml/3½fl oz/generous ⅓ cup mirin
45ml/3 tbsp granulated sugar
100ml/3½fl oz/generous ⅓ cup soy
   sauce

For the seasoning

200ml/7fl oz/scant 1 cup kombu and
   bonito stock or instant dashi
100ml/3½fl oz/generous ⅓ cup sake
15ml/1 tbsp soy sauce

1 To make sukiyaki stock, bring the mirin to the boil. Add the sugar and soy sauce and bring to the boil again, then remove from the heat and set aside.

2 To make the seasoning, bring the stock, sake and soy sauce to the boil, then remove from the heat and set aside.

3 Arrange the separated beef slices on a large serving plate. Set the lard for cooking on the same plate. Place all the remaining ingredients, except the eggs, on large plates.

4 Stand the portable cooker on a suitably heavy mat to protect the dining table and ensure that it can be heated safely. Melt the lard, add three or four slices of beef and some leeks or spring onions, and then pour in the sukiyaki stock. Gradually add all the remaining ingredients, except the eggs, to the cooker.

5 Beat an egg in a small bowl for each person.

6 When the beef and vegetables are cooked, diners help themselves to the ingredients and dip them in the raw egg.

7 Gradually add the seasoning when the stock has thickened and carry on cooking until the ingredients have all been eaten. If required, add additional sugar and soy sauce to taste for extra flavour.

Seafood and Pork Pancakes

INGREDIENTS

Serves 4
320g/11¹/₂oz/scant 4 cups green
  cabbage, finely shredded
135ml/9 tbsp bonito flakes
bunch of spring onions, finely sliced
oil, for cooking
12 raw tiger prawns, shelled
8 baby squid, cleaned and sliced
200g/7oz boneless pork belly
salt and black pepper
mayonnaise and ginger pickles, to
  garnish

For the batter
4 size 2 eggs
275ml/9fl oz/generous 1 cup water
275g/10oz/2¹/₂ cups plain flour
10ml/2 tsp baking powder

For the okonomiyaki sauce
30ml/2 tbsp tomato ketchup
15ml/1 tbsp Worcestershire sauce
7.5ml/1¹/₂ tsp granulated sugar

1 First make the batter: beat the eggs until frothy, then stir in the water. Gradually sift in the flour and baking powder and mix until smooth.

2 Mix about 40g/1¹/₂oz/¹/₂ cup cabbage and 15ml/1 tbsp bonito flakes in a large bowl. Reserve some of the spring onions for serving, then add an eighth of the remainder to the cabbage. Stir in an eighth of the batter.

3 Mix the ingredients for the okonomiyaki sauce. Place a portable cooker on a thick mat on the table and heat a little oil over a high heat. Cook a quarter of the prawns and squid with a little salt and pepper, then set aside. Reduce the heat and pour in the cabbage mixture, then place the cooked prawns and squid on the pancake and cook for 2–3 minutes, or until the underneath of the pancake has set and browned.

4 Use two spatulas to turn the pancake over and cook the second side for 2–3 minutes, then turn it again.

5 Top with a little okonomiyaki sauce, mayonnaise, spring onions and ginger pickles, then serve. Garnish with extra bonito flakes. Repeat, making three more fish pancakes.

6 Thinly slice the pork, then cook four pork pancakes in the same way as for the prawn.

Assorted Tempura

INGREDIENTS

Serves 4–6
1 quantity Tempura Dip
115g/4oz finely grated mooli (daikon
  `radish), (optional)
115g/4oz sweet potato, unpeeled, sliced
  and soaked in cold water for
  5 minutes
75g/3oz carrot, cut into matchsticks
4 shiitake mushrooms, stems removed
50g/2oz/³/₄ cup French beans, trimmed
1 red pepper, seeded and sliced into
  2cm/³/₄in thick strips
¹/₂ squid body sack, cut into 3cm/1¹/₄in
  thick strips
8 large tiger prawns, prepared as for
  Prawn Tempura
1 quantity Tempura Batter
oil, for deep frying
flour, for coating

1 Make the Tempura Dip, then leave to cool and strain. Divide it between four small bowls. Place the grated mooli (if using) in a fine sieve and set aside to drain.

2 When all the vegetables and seafood are prepared, make the batter following the recipe instructions.

3 Heat the oil for deep frying to 185°C/365°F.

4 Dust the prawns lightly with flour and, holding them by the tail, quickly dip them into the batter, then slowly lower them into the oil. Fry all the prawns and squid in this way, then reduce the temperature of the oil to 170°C/340°F.

5 Dip the vegetables straight into the batter and cook in the same way. Dip the carrots and beans in small bunches. Dip only the undersides of the mushrooms. Drain well. If the batter begins to thin, sprinkle 15ml/ 1 tbsp flour over it without mixing.

6 Place the tempura on a plate and serve immediately with the dip.

Chicken and Prawn Hot Pot

Using a portable hot pot, this dish, known as *Yosenabe*, combines meat, fish, vegetables and noodles to create a really warming meal that is cooked at the table.

INGREDIENTS

Serves 4

400g/14oz chicken thigh or breast on
the bone
8 raw tiger prawns
200g/7oz dried udon noodles
4 shiitake mushrooms, stems removed
½ bunch Chinese leaves, cut into
3cm/1¼in slices
3 leeks, sliced diagonally into pieces
1cm/½in thick
15 x 10cm/6 x 4in piece tofu (about
150g/5oz), cut into 3cm/1¼in cubes
300g/11oz shirataki noodles, boiled for
2 minutes, drained and halved

For the yosenabe stock

1 litre/1¾ pints/4 cups kombu and
bonito stock
90ml/6 tbsp sake or dry white wine
30ml/2 tbsp soy sauce
20ml/4 tsp mirin
10ml/2 tsp salt

1 Cut the chicken into 3–4cm/
1¼–1½in chunks. Remove the black intestinal vein from the prawns (see below).

2 Cook the udon for 2 minutes less than the packet instructions, drain and wash thoroughly, then drain again and set aside.

> — COOK'S TIP —
>
> To remove the black vein from the back of an unpeeled prawn, bend the prawn and use a bamboo skewer or cocktail stick to lift out the vein from between the joins in the shell. Do this about a third of the way along the back of the prawn.

3 Arrange all the remaining ingredients on large plates.

4 Bring all the ingredients for the yosenabe stock to the boil in the hot pot. Add the chicken and simmer for 3 minutes, skimming the broth throughout cooking.

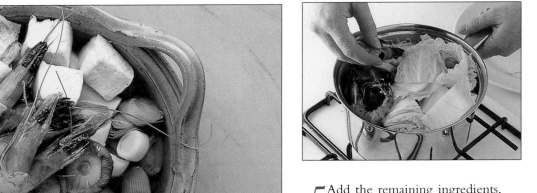

5 Add the remaining ingredients, except the udon noodles, and simmer for 5 minutes or until cooked.

6 Diners serve themselves from the simmering hot pot. Finally, when all the ingredients have been eaten, add the udon noodles to the rest of the soup, heat through and serve in bowls to round off the meal.

Serve-yourself Sushi

This is a fun dish, known as *Temaki-zushi*, for which every diner selects favourite ingredients, wraps them in seaweed and dips them in soy sauce. Sometimes mayonnaise is added to the filling to make it even more tasty.

INGREDIENTS

Serves 4
480g/1lb 1oz/2¹/₅ cups Japanese rice, cooked as for Shaped Sushi, using Mixed Vinegar below

For the Mixed Vinegar
60ml/4 tbsp rice vinegar
30ml/2 tbsp sugar
5ml/1 tsp salt

For the Rolled Omelette
2 size 1 eggs
10ml/2 tsp sugar
pinch of salt

For the fillings
115g/4oz block tuna for sashimi
115g/4oz block salmon for sashimi
4–8 crab sticks
1 squid body sack, skinned (about 200g/7oz total weight)
¹/₂ cucumber, seeds removed
1 avocado, halved, stoned and peeled
juice of ¹/₂ lemon
4–8 raw tiger prawns, prepared as for Shaped Sushi
60ml/4 tbsp salmon roe
¹/₂ round lettuce, separated into leaves
punnet of cress, trimmed
wasabi
mayonnaise
10 sheets yaki-nori seaweed, quartered, for rolling
soy sauce, to serve

1 Make one Rolled Omelette using the ingredients listed above.

2 Slice the tuna, salmon, crab sticks and squid into 1cm/¹/₂in square long strips.

3 Cut the cucumber, avocado and omelette into similar-sized strips. Sprinkle lemon juice on the avocado.

4 Place all the ingredients on platters, the rice in a bowl and the seaweed on a separate plate.

5 Each guest takes a piece of seaweed and lays it flat with the shiny side facing downwards. About 15ml/1 tbsp rice is placed on the nori seaweed and spread evenly with the fingers. Selected topping ingredients to taste are placed neatly on the middle of the rice in strips, wasabi or mayonnaise added to taste and the nori rolled up into small tubes. The impromptu sushi are dipped in soy sauce and eaten. Diners keep going until all the prepared ingredients are eaten.

Index